Annette Wolter

Cockatiels

How to Take Care of Them and Understand Them

With color photographs by Karin Skogstad and other animal photographers

Illustrations by György Jankovics

Consulting Editor: Matthew M. Vriends, PhD

BARRON'S

Contents

Preface

When a tame cockatiel looks around with an enterprising air and raises its crest jauntily, it is signaling that it is ready to play with its human owner. Now is the moment to take some time for your pet, for a bird that is kept singly needs a lot of attention and affection from its keeper. If you don't have much time to spare for your pet, you'll be better off getting two cockatiels. But whether you have one or more of these popular birds, the important thing is to know how to provide them with the environment and the care that meet their natural needs.

You will find out just what is required in this pet owner's manual by cockatiel expert Annette Wolter. She explains in simple terms what to look for when buying a bird, what kind of cage and accessories to get, how to feed cockatiels properly, and what to do if your bird gets sick. In addition, she offers practical advice on how to win your cockatiel's trust and some promising suggestions for teaching your bird how to speak and whistle. The concrete and easy-to-follow instructions make it possible for children, too, to understand and take care of a cockatiel of their own.

Charming color photos by outstanding bird photographers and informative drawings convey vivid pictures of these small parrots, which contribute so much fun to a household with their affectionate personalities.

The author of this book and the editors of Barron's Pet Owner's Manuals wish you much happiness with your cockatiel.

Cockatiels need company. A single bird that is left alone too much may develop into a screamer, start plucking its own feathers, or pine away and ultimately die of frustrated longing for a companion. If you don't have much time for your pet, you should get a pair of cockatiels.

Please read "Important Note" on page 63.

Think Before You Buy

A cockatiel, like all creatures, develops its own particular personality. In your daily dealings with the bird you will soon find out what it likes and dislikes and become familiar with its different patterns of behavior.

The Nature of Cockatiels

Cockatiels are not excitable, high-spirited birds; rather, they are quite deliberate in their ways. Their somewhat shrill voices may strike some people as unpleasant, but a contented bird resorts to its voice only occasionally to emit a warning or an alarm and is more likely to use it for whistling, imitating noises, or mimicking some words it hears a lot. Young cockatiels can become very tame and trusting. They grow into lovable companions that quickly overcome their initial, often panicky fearfulness and form deep attachments to the people they know well. Although cockatiels like to be active, their play is not as amusing as, say, that of a parakeet. A cockatiel is quite content if it has something to work on with its beak, branches to gnaw on, or a piece of cardboard or other object to reduce to shreds.

Naturally, a cage for a cockatiel takes up more room than one for a parakeet. A cockatiel also needs considerably more space for flying than its smaller, much more agile relative. In addition, a cockatiel creates more dust than most other pet birds because it keeps growing new down feathers, the tips of which disintegrate into a fine dust that impregnates the rest of the plumage.

To decide whether a cockatiel would be happy with you and whether you would feel constrained by the bird's presence, here are ten questions you should ponder.

Ten Questions to Help You Decide

1. A properly kept cockatiel lives about 15 years. Are you prepared to care for it that long?

2. Do you have a good and permanent spot for a rather large cage (see page 11)?

3. Will you be able to let the bird fly free every day?

4. Do you have enough time to devote to the bird?

5. Is someone available to play with it, talk to it, and whistle to it?

6. What will happen to the bird when you want to go away on vacation?

7. Are there other pets in your household that might not get along with the bird? You can teach a dog that the bird is a member of the family, but a cat will not understand.

8. Are you thinking of giving the bird to a child? If so, the ultimate responsibility for the cockatiel's well-being will still be yours because children can lose interest in a bird quickly.

9. Are you sure that no one in the family is allergic to bird feathers and feather dust? (See Important Note, page 63.)

10. Are you keeping in mind that the bird's food and health requirements will cost money on an ongoing basis?

Conflicts arise even between cockatiels that ▶ *get along well together. Here the bird on the right is telling the other, "My turn now!"*

Male or Female?

If you are looking for a single cockatiel, you don't need to worry about the bird's sex. Young males and females adjust equally well to life with people—whether one person or a family—become tame, try to whistle or talk, and develop their own idiosyncrasies. However, if you hope for offspring from your birds, you should get the advice of an experienced breeder or pet dealer to be sure that the second bird you select is the proper sexual counterpart of the first one.

Sexing young cockatiels is something only an experienced breeder or dealer can do with any degree of certainty. Before the post-juvenile molt, the orange cheek patch of the male is no brighter than that of the female, and the characteristic markings on the under tail-coverts of the female haven't shown up. I know several cockatiels with names like Chico, Mike, or Tony whose owners found an egg in the cage after a couple of years—evidence that the supposed male was in fact a female.

Sexing adult cockatiels, that is, birds that have passed through their post-juvenile molt at about nine months, presents no difficulty. The plumage gives a clear indication of a bird's sex. The contrasting colors are paler in the female than in the male. The cheek spot and the mask, that is, the facial areas that stand out from the gray ground color, look, in the female, as though they had been dusted with a brownish powder. The female also has yellow and black crossbanding on the under tail-coverts, and there is some yellowish white on the rims of the outer tail feathers, which are all gray in the male.

Extending one leg and the wing of the same side simultaneously is a gesture of relaxation and resembles our stretching in physical comfort.

One Bird or a Pair?

Most people want just one cockatiel, on the assumption that a single bird will be friendlier and will more readily learn to whistle or even talk. What they don't think about is that a single, caged cockatiel will be happy only if a human is willing to make up for the lack of avian company by being around a lot of the time and paying plenty of attention to the bird.

For me, the ideal solution is always to get a pair. Start out, however, with one bird. Once the youngster has learned to trust you, you can get it a companion. Because the first bird has learned to enjoy whistling, talking, and playing all sorts of tricks, it will not lose interest in these activities. The new bird will initially concentrate all its attention on the other bird and will regard the human members of the household with timid suspicion rather than affection. But it will learn quickly from its model, the other cockatiel, just how "useful" these humans can be.

It doesn't matter, by the way, whether or not the two birds belong to opposite sexes—unless you hope for offspring from them. If two male or two female cockatiels are kept together, one of them automatically assumes the role of the absent sex. A relationship between such a couple is disrupted only if a third cockatiel appears on the scene. Keeping three birds is always an ordeal for one of them and should be avoided.

The Colors of the Plumage

The Australian ancestors of our cage-bred cockatiels are of a delicate gray color that sometimes has a bluish or brownish tinge. The upper tail-coverts are silver gray; the lower tail-coverts, blackish gray. White feathers on the outer secondaries form a striking band on the wings. Throat, cheeks, and forehead are a bright lemon yellow, against which the deep orange feathers in the ear region show up clearly, forming the so-called cheek patch below the black eyes. The feathers of the crest rise from the yellow forehead. The shorter ones forming the front of the crest are yellow; the longer back ones are gray like the crown but have some pale yellow barbs intermingled with the gray. The crest of a cockatiel is considerably more slender than that of a cockatoo. A fine line of gray feathers runs from the brownish gray cere above the strong, gray beak toward the eyes, cutting across the mask between the bright yellow forehead and the more delicately colored lower half of the face, which becomes white farther down.

Color variants created through selective breeding include albinos, lutinos, pieds, pearled (laced or opaline), cinnamons, silvers, and white-face

(charcoal) (see below for descriptions). These are only the best known varieties; there are all kinds of combinations of these colors. To describe them all would be beyond the scope of this book.

Albinos are white but retain the yellow mask and orange cheek patches. The color of the feet varies from dark to light gray, and the lower tail-coverts are light yellow in male and bright yellow in female birds. Both sexes of pure albinos have red eyes. The many white birds with black eyes are, from the breeder's point of view, not pure albinos.

Lutinos are white, tinged all over with an even, delicate yellow. Their eyes are normally red but can also be black.

Pied (**harlequin** or **variegated**) cockatiels have irregular white patches. There are also pieds in different color combinations. Some of these birds look almost black because they are dark gray all over. The mask and cheek spot form a striking contrast to the rest of the bird.

Pearled (**laced** or **opaline**) cockatiels have white and yellow, pearly markings on the feathers of the back and on the wing coverts.

A metal mirror is tough enough to withstand attacks from a cockatiel's strong beak.

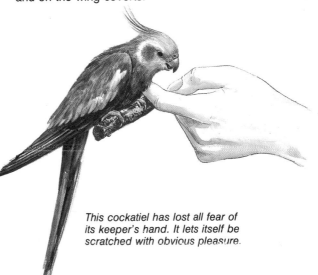

This cockatiel has lost all fear of its keeper's hand. It lets itself be scratched with obvious pleasure.

7

Cinnamon (**fawn** or **isabelle**) cockatiels are, as the name implies, a cinnamon brown.

In **silver** cockatiels the plumage is a lighter brownish gray with what looks like a silver dusting. These birds have red eyes.

Finally, **white-heads** or **charcoals** are cockatiels that look like their wild relatives but lack the yellow mask and reddish cheeks.

My tip: All these carefully bred strains may look very attractive, but experience has shown that these birds are more susceptible to disease than naturally colored cockatiels.

The Right Place for the Cage

If your cockatiel is to feel comfortable and safe, it needs a fairly large

Male or female? This question is immaterial if you want only one bird. Birds of both sexes become friendly and can learn to talk. Cockatiels with a gift for speech mimic many phrases they hear frequently.

This white-head is watching attentively what is going on.

cage (see "The Right Cage," page 11) set up in a permanent place.

The best place is the living room because there the bird can most often see the family with whom it is going to live and can get acquainted with all its members—at first from a safe distance. The cage should be located in a bright corner near a window. The corner should not be so crowded, however, that people have to pass by too close to the cage; such human proximity is frightening to a cockatiel that is still shy. Perhaps you have a piece of furniture, not too tall, that could serve as a stand for the cage. Better yet, because it is less subject to vibrations, would be a wide shelf on the wall, mounted securely at about eye level. If a bird can see people's faces, it is least likely to be shy. The space above the cage should be open because birds respond with fear to activity above their heads. Something stable to climb on, such as a sturdy forked branch, should be mounted on top of the cage to serve as perch and landing spot when the bird flies free.

Very important: The place for the cage must be absolutely draft-free. Even slight drafts can make cockatiels sick. Check with a lit candle whether there are drafts. The flame will flicker at air movements that we are quite unaware of.

Unsuitable locations

• A spot directly in front of a window: In the winter too much cold enters, and in the summer it is too hot.
• The kitchen: Everything in a kitchen is dangerous—vapors, hot burners, pots with liquid or hot contents, detergents, cleansers, and other substances that are poisonous to birds.
• A child's room: Here life is too boring because children are away at school or play or have to do homework most of the day, and then it's time to go to bed.

These three birds show how different the plumages of various cockatiels can look.

In the photo: *Even breeders disagree whether the bird on the left should be described as "pearled" or "rimmed." The other two present no such problems: The middle one is an albino; the one on the right, a pied cockatiel.*

Tips for Buying a Bird

Where You Can Get Cockatiels

At pet stores: Here you can usually choose from among several birds of various colors.

From cockatiel breeders: Breeders prefer to sell their birds directly to private individuals because they like to make sure that the birds they have raised with loving care will have good homes. You can get names and addresses of breeders through bird clubs or from animal shelters. You may well have to pick up your cockatiel from the breeder. Never have a bird shipped to you. A bird mailed in a box will be badly frightened and may be subjected to rough handling.

Note: When you buy a cockatiel, ask for a formal bill of sale. It should include the following information: date of purchase, kind of bird, number on the band (see page 11), price, and addresses of the buyer and seller.

The perches in the cage and on the bird tree must be thick enough so that the cockatiel's toes cannot reach all the way around. The claws should not meet.

Shopping List

A cage as described on page 11
A birdseed mixture designed for cockatiels, preferably the kind the bird is used to
Spray millet
A mineral stone or cuttlebone
Activated charcoal for treating diarrhea
One or two extra food cups
Corn cob or cage paper
A brass bell on a short, solid chain
A swing with a wooden perch
For a single bird, a metal mirror
Other toys (see page 28), preferably made of wood

What to Consider When Buying

The bird's age is important: A young bird, about 10 to 12 weeks old, adjusts best to people and will become tame quickly if treated properly. But remember that the plumage of all young cockatiels is still pale; males don't develop their full color until they are about nine months old.

How to tell a young cockatiel
- The cheek spot is apparent but not yet bright orange.
- The outer edges of the tail feathers have thin, whitish to yellow edges.
- The tail is somewhat shorter than that of a fully grown cockatiel.
- The cere is still pink.
- The movements of juvenile birds are still quite clumsy.

What a healthy cockatiel looks like
- All the feathers are fully formed, hug the body smoothly, and have a lustrous sheen.
- The feathers around the cloaca, that is the bird's anus, are not sticky or smeared with feces.
- There is no discharge, either runny or dried into crusts, from the eyes and nostrils.
- The two middle toes on the feet point forward, the two outer ones, back; there are no missing toes.
- The bird moves normally, has contact with the other birds, and preens itself.

What a sick cockatiel looks like
A sick bird sits by itself apathetically, with puffed-up plumage and half-shut eyes. The beak is buried in the back feathers. However, not every cockatiel that fits this description is sick. This is also the sleep posture of

When a cockatiel wants to groom its back feathers, it has to turn its head 180 degrees.

do not keep large cages in stock and have to place special orders for them. In such cases it may take several days for the cage to arrive.

My tip: Buy the cage early enough to have it ready and all set up when you bring your bird home (see "Setting Up the Cage Properly," page 13).

healthy birds, and cockatiels often take short naps during the day.

Note: Cockatiels are not among the parrots listed in CITES. This means that, apart from the bill of sale, no special papers are needed when you buy your bird.

A Suitable Cage

No cage should be the constant abode of a cockatiel, for these birds have to be able to fly or they will become obese and sick. Even if you allow the bird as much flying time as possible, however, it will still have to spend many hours in the cage (whenever you air or clean the room, for example, or have social gatherings). For this reason the cage has to be at least large enough for the cockatiel to extend its wings sideward and upward without touching the cage bars, and to move about without the tail brushing against the perches. Many pet dealers

The Right Cockatiel Cage	
Material:	Metal cage and door, with a bottom and a tray of unbreakable plastic
Size:	Ideal dimensions: 40 × 28 × 52 inches (10 × 70 × 132 cm) (for one or two birds); minimum dimensions: 23 × 14 × 30 inches (58 × 34 × 74 cm) (for 1 bird)
Bars:	Running horizontally on the long walls so that the bird can climb up and down on them
Spacing of bars:	½–1 inch (1½–2½ cm) apart
Perches:	Three or four hardwood dowels, ¾ inch (20 mm) thick, or, even better, tree branches of various thicknesses, ½–1 inch (14–26 mm)
Food and water cups:	At least two dishes, to be hung on the bars, for birdseed and raw food; one water dispenser or drinking cup without a cover

The Band

The cockatiel you buy will probably be wearing a band on its leg with a registered number stamped on it. This band is proof that the bird comes from

This cage is large enough to house two cockatiels.

an aviculturist who is a member of a cockatiel society. The number on the band is registered by both the breeder and the society. Since cockatiels can usually be entered in an exhibition only if they are banded, you may want to keep the band on. But check the "ringed" leg frequently, for bands have caused many mishaps. If the band gets caught on something, for instance, the bird will keep pulling to get free and may injure itself in the process. If the leg then swells up, circulation to the leg and foot is impeded. If this happens, the band must be promptly removed by the pet dealer or a veterinarian. Be sure to retain the band and to keep it in a safe place because it represents important evidence of the bird's origin.

Gentle Acclimation

The New Home

Bring your cockatiel, packed in its box, home as quickly as possible, taking care to protect it from cold, dampness, and heat. When you arrive home, the cage should be all ready for its new occupant and set up in its permanent place. If things aren't quite ready, the bird should stay in its cardboard prison a bit longer, for once it has entered its cage, nobody should reach a hand in for the rest of the day. Also, no changes should be made in the cage for the next few days.

Setting Up the Cage Properly

• If the cage comes equipped with plastic perches, or even wooden dowels, these should be removed and replaced with tree branches of the right thickness (see page 22). Squeeze the ends of the branches between the cage bars or tie them into place with raffia.
• Supply at most one more branch than there were perches in the cage.
• Mount the branches so that three of them are horizontal, the others at an angle. In nature, birds don't always sit on horizontal branches.
• Don't place the branches directly above the food and water cups. If you do, droppings may land in the bird's seed or water.
• Spread about ⅜ inch (1 cm) of corn cob in the tray at the bottom.
• Fill one cup with birdseed, one with water, and one with washed, coarsely grated carrot or apple.
• Attach a piece of spray millet to the cage grating with a clothespin, or in-

sert it in a special holder you can buy at a pet store (see drawing, page 40). The spray of millet should be easily accessible from one of the branches.
• Fasten the mineral stone or cuttlebone to the cage bars with the wire supplied in the package. The stone, too, should be near a perch.
• Hang a little bell above one of the upper branches.

It may take several weeks for your cockatiel to overcome its fear of you. Don't lose patience! Eventually the bird will learn to trust you completely.

If you want your cockatiel to climb onto your finger, press the finger gently against the bird's abdomen in a horizontal position.

My tip: Make sure you have a good supply of raffia, because the bird will nibble on it, and it will have to be replaced periodically.

The Move into the Cage

Remember that your cockatiel is probably still in a state of shock. Being caught, banded, separated from its companions, and transported were highly traumatic experiences for it. Under no circumstances should you attempt to reach into the box for the bird. If you did, you would make painful acquaintance with its strong beak, and the bird would form and remember an image of you as a dangerous enemy. Instead, hold the opened transport box in front of the cage door in such a way that the only way out is into the cage. Since the bird will want to get out of its dark box toward the light, it will move into the cage without outside urging.

Important: As soon as the bird is out of the box, shut the cage door and move away.

The First Hours at Home

Leave the bird completely undisturbed at first, so that it can inspect its cage and other surroundings in peace and get used to them.

Wait several hours or until the next day before sitting down at some distance from the cage but close enough so that the bird can see you. Talk to it and repeatedly pronounce its name, which you will have chosen ahead of time. After just a few days the bird will realize that the name has something to do with it and will respond by producing a sound of its own, shaking its plumage, or raising its wings. You will know that it has recovered from the shock of being relocated when it no longer sits in the same spot as though glued there but starts moving back and forth a little and examining its quarters more closely.

My tip: If the bird keeps sitting in the same place for hours, approach it very gently, speaking to it in a soothing voice, and offer it a few sunflower

Damp leaves in a shallow dish will enable a cockatiel to take a dew bath, just as in nature. Many birds love such baths above all else.

seeds on a long stick. The way to do this is to cut a notch in one end of the stick and jam the kernels loosely into the notch. Often such an offer is the beginning of a long-lasting friendship between a bird and its keeper.

Night Rest Is Important

Cockatiels that are not yet used to their new surroundings are very easily frightened. Especially at night, unfamiliar noises can make them panic, and they can get hurt when they flutter around frantically in the cage. For this reason you should leave a small light on during the first few nights. If the bird can orient itself visually, it will not react with the same violent movements when it gets frightened.

My tip: Don't cover the cage with a cloth at night. Being unable to see, the bird may get frightened for even the slightest reason and begin to thrash around wildly.

Bedtime for the cockatiel: Once your bird has become acclimated, it will decide for itself when to go to bed. At the beginning you can induce sleepiness by dimming the light and playing soft music or talking quietly. Even if the television is on, the bird won't be bothered as long as the sound is not too loud and the screen is not directly in the bird's line of vision.

A set sleeping spot: Later, when your cockatiel has become acclimated to life with you, you will notice that it always settles down in the same place when bedtime approaches. Or perhaps the bird will have two or three favorite sleeping spots. Make sure, before you turn off the light, that it is perched in one of these locations because in the dark it may not be able to find the right place and may panic.

The First Days at Home

The morning after the first night your cockatiel spends with you will bring new excitement for you and your bird because now you may have to reach into the cage to replenish the food. When you do, speak softly to the bird and avoid abrupt, hasty movements. Don't be afraid of the big beak—the bird is still too frightened to use it in self-defense. It will undoubtedly slide into the farthest corner of its cage to get as far away as possible from your hand. When done with the morning chores, avoid reaching into the cage unnecessarily for the first few days, until the bird begins to realize that this human hand is a source of food.

How to encourage the bird to trust you

• Always speak to the bird in a soft voice when you have to do anything in or near the cage. Say its name, keep whistling the same short tunes, or repeat the same short sentences.
• Don't be frightened if the bird pecks at you; it doesn't have enough courage yet to really bite.
• A cockatiel that feels afraid hisses. If you hear this sound, stop what you are doing and try again later.
• Try to do the routine chores at the same time every day.

What a bird finds frightening: As long as your cockatiel is still shy, you should not change anything in or near its cage. Don't, for instance, move the food cups to a new place, and don't put unfamiliar objects down near the bird. You should also avoid making drastic changes in your own appearance; now is not the time to introduce aviator sunglasses or a large, floppy hat.

How to help your bird to get used to new things: You would, of course, like to feed your cockatiel as varied a diet as possible. But it may refuse to touch a piece of unfamiliar fruit or vegetable for days because it is afraid of it. There is only one thing to do:

keep on offering the unfamiliar item. You can try eating a piece yourself in the bird's presence; perhaps that will stir your cockatiel's curiosity.

It will also take quite a long time for the bird to get used to your hand. At first the hand is seen as a threat, but if it is experienced day after day as a source of food, the bird will begin to accept it. Try offering a few seeds on the back of your hand every day after refilling the dishes.

Many cockatiels enjoy being sprayed with lukewarm water from a plant mister. They raise their wings and twist and turn to expose all parts of the body to the water.

Making the Bird Hand-tame

As soon as your cockatiel dares take a few seeds from your hand, it is time to ask more of it.

The first step: Use your finger to scratch the bird's abdomen very gently. If the bird moves away, follow it cautiously with your hand.

Daily preening is a must.

The tail is groomed as thoroughly

The second step: After the daily scratching, hand the cockatiel an unpainted wooden curtain ring. When the ring drops to the cage floor after the bird is through working on it with its beak, pick it up and remove it so it will continue to hold interest for the bird.

The third step: At some point, following the daily scratching, press your finger gently but firmly against the bird's abdominal feathers, quite low down. Hold the finger horizontally. Perhaps the bird will climb up on it. If it does, give it the wooden ring to gnaw on. After a few days you will be able to lift your cockatiel out of its cage on your finger and let it have its first experience of flying free—but more about that later (see "The First Flight," page 19).

My tip: Always offer the bird your finger or the back of your hand to perch on. Most birds are frightened by an open, upturned hand.

Avoid at all cost: Never try to grasp the bird, let alone catch it in midair. There is no worse thing for a bird than to be grasped. This would severely shake the trust in your hand that you have patiently built up.

Getting Used to Bathing

Offer your bird a chance to bathe about every three days. Many pet cockatiels enjoy baths even though cockatiels don't bathe in the wild; the most they do is to let their plumage get moistened by the rain. In the dry air of heated rooms, however, many cockatiels welcome an opportunity for bathing.

. . as the wings.

. . . and not a single feather is neglected.

A full bath: Some cockatiels readily take advantage of an opportunity to take a full bath when it presents itself. Fill a large, shallow dish with lukewarm water, and place it in front of the cage. Cockatiels that take baths like to dip their outstretched wings in the water and get their heads wet.

A dew bath: This makes sense if your cockatiel is reluctant to take a full bath. Place some wet leaves, such as dandelion greens, chickweed, spinach, or young leaves from trees, in a large, shallow dish. Your bird will delight in playing around in the damp greens because cockatiels are used to dew baths in nature, where they forage for food in grass wet with morning dew.

My tip: Don't use lettuce for these baths because most lettuce is sprayed with chemicals. These dissolve in the water and are harmful to birds.

Showers: Many cockatiels are fond of showers, for which you can use a plant mister (see drawing, page 15). If the bird is enjoying this lukewarm shower bath, it will expose all parts of its body to the water. If, however, it responds fearfully by trying to avoid the spray, don't persist at this particular time. Even if your cockatiel shows no initial enthusiasm for a full bath, a dew bath, or a shower, you should continue to offer one or another of these opportunities for bathing.

Important: Make very sure that the plant mister has never been used with plant pesticides.

Life with a Cockatiel

The full reality of life with your cockatiel doesn't set in until the day the bird leaves its cage for the first time to fly free in the room. This event should be carefully prepared for because cockatiels fly very fast, and a pet bird needs to get used to the space restrictions gradually. As a general rule, birds quickly learn to judge the size of a room accurately and then to make the most of their limited freedom. Above all, the cockatiel is now able to satisfy its curiosity and to examine at close range many things that looked intriguing from the cage. All shiny objects wherein the bird can see even a partial reflection of itself will be very attractive to it. Small objects will be picked up in the beak and carried

This cockatiel feels so relaxed on its keeper's hand that it is cleaning its toes, completely oblivious to where it is.

around, and the bird will spend quite a bit of time marching around on the floor and on tables. Unfortunately, it will also leave traces behind that will have to be cleaned up. For this reason you should set up a place in the room that is congenial to the bird and where it will spend the major part of its time out of the cage.

Important: At first, let your cockatiel out of its cage only under your supervision. Don't leave it alone even for a couple of hours until you are quite familiar with its habits and preferences and until the room is really safe for the bird.

Flying Without Danger

Before you open the cage door, all the windows must be closed or at least screened; even casement windows will not prevent a bird from escaping. The doors to the room must be shut, too, for the bird should get to know one room before it encounters others.

Very dangerous for birds are windows without curtains or shades. Birds don't recognize glass as a barrier and will fly into it with such speed that they may break their necks or sustain other severe injuries. If there are no curtains, get some shades or venetian blinds and lower them until only a few inches at the bottom remain uncovered. Also turn on the electric light. Then increase the covered area of the window a little every day until the bird has realized that the window is an invisible wall. This process usually doesn't take more than a few days, and the same method can then be used in other rooms.

The First Flight

When you open the cage door for the first time, your cockatiel may stare out of the barless opening entranced but make no move to get out. After all, this is a totally new situation. Probably the bird has never flown before. In the nest box things were too crowded, and in the dealer's or breeder's community cage it probably couldn't do much more than flap its wings.

Give it time: At some point the curiosity to explore the surroundings close up will become too great to resist. Perhaps the cockatiel will start by climbing on top of its cage. Instead, it may get onto your finger to be lifted out; set the bird down on the cage. From there it will take off and start practicing its inborn flying abilities.

Landing maneuvers: Landing is another skill your cockatiel has not yet had a chance to practice and that has to be learned. The bird will instinctively try to land either on the floor or on as high a spot as possible. If it succeeds in landing on its cage, this is sheer luck. Leave it up to the bird to either climb back inside or take another sweep through the room. The cockatiel may also land on a lamp, a curtain rod, or a tall piece of furniture and will then be reluctant to fly back to the cage.

Luring the bird into the cage: If your bird lands on the floor, sprinkle some seeds there for it. Cockatiels love to forage for food on the ground, and your bird will realize that you mean it well. If you now put the cage near it on the floor, it will probably be quite relieved to climb back in. It is harder to persuade a bird to return to the cage from a high perch because it feels secure where it is, but don't lose your patience. Talk to the bird encouragingly, and try to lure it with a millet spray. Or, after about a half hour, hold the open cage up to it; maybe it will be happy to climb in. If not, let your cockatiel sit on its high perch. Sooner or later it will get hungry and return to the cage, although this may not happen until the next morning.

Avoid at all cost: Don't try to chase the bird, especially not by waving cloths or a broom at it. Such pursuit would instantly destroy all the trust that has been built up.

Thanks to its flexibility and control of body movements, a cockatiel can reach almost everywhere for preening.

Cockatiels Have Their Favorite "Hangouts"

The more adept your cockatiel becomes at maneuvering around the room, the more eager it will be to get out of its cage and spend time in its favorite spots. And you will soon notice that the bird, once there, is not idle but starts, at first tentatively and then more and more intently, to gnaw on wood, wallpaper, or curtains. Although cockatiels gnaw much less

Keeping a pair of cockatiels not only gives you a chance to observe the charming behavior of the birds toward each other but also allows you to leave the house for a few hours or even days without feeling guilty.

than other parrots, they cannot live without exercising their beaks.

I made my first acquaintance with cockatiels when I lived in an apartment that was not exactly ideal for keeping birds. The owners of this particular pair of cockatiels had to travel abroad unexpectedly for some time and were very relieved to find someone willing to take their birds. Charlie and Laura were inseparable and very tame. Both clearly enjoyed flying in my two connected rooms without a door between them. Soon they had established where they liked to settle down for a rest, and they satisfied their urge to keep busy by working on the curtains. These were soon punctuated with many holes, luckily in not very obvious places. At that point I bought the biggest Christmas wreath made out of straw I could find and hung it where there was plenty of empty space underneath it. Then I spread a piece of heavy, clear plastic on the floor below. From one moment to the next Charlie and Laura moved from their work area on the curtains to the wreath, which kept them both busy for over six months, when they were picked up by their owners. A little "bird island" like this in the room also cuts down on the negative impact birds have on the furniture and thus helps their owners to relax. A bird tree, of course, makes a much longer lasting "island" than a straw wreath, meets a cockatiel's urge to gnaw and to climb much better, and also has enough room to accommodate a second bird.

The Bird Tree

Bird stands with perches consisting of natural branches are now available for cockatiels at pet stores and are ideal for people who don't enjoy making things themselves. A bird stand with wooden dowels as perches can be used as the basic structure for a bird tree, and a stand on rollers has the great advantage that it can easily be moved out of the way for cleaning. It doesn't matter whether you start with such a bird stand or with a plastic tub (of the sort used for hydroculture) as the basis of your bird tree—just be sure that the branches you are going to incorporate are not from the wrong trees.

Use nonpoisonous branches: Branches from fruit trees are ideal if you are absolutely sure they haven't been sprayed with pesticides. If there is any doubt, you had better use twigs and branches from other trees such as oak, alder, basswood, common privet, poplar, or willow. Even here, however, caution is in order: don't gather the branches along roads be-

A picture of a bird tree, showing the inside of the outer tub. Such a "haven" in your living room will quickly become your cockatiel's favorite "hang-out."

Dangers For a Cockatiel

Danger	How to Avoid
Bathroom: Bird may escape through a casement window, or drown in the toilet.	Keep the bathroom door shut. Let the bird in only if you are present.
Open doors: Tops are used as perches; toes are squashed if door is closed.	Always check where the bird is before you shut a door.
Floor: Bird playing on the floor may be killed if someone steps on it.	Get used to treading very cautiously.
Vessels containing water: Bird may slip into a bucket, bowl, big glass, or vase and drown (soap suds are mistaken for a landing surface).	Cover vessels, and don't let the bird fly free while you clean.
Closets, open drawers: Bird may inadvertently be locked in and may suffocate or starve to death.	Never leave closets or drawers open, not even a crack.
Poisons: Fatal poisoning can be caused by alcohol, pencil lead, magic markers, ballpoint pens, strong spices, verdigris, glues, varnishes, solvents, fertilizers, plastic wrap, cleansers, mercury, heavily scented sprays, detergents, and thick cigarette smoke.	Store all items listed where the bird cannot get at them. Remove all traces of them after use. Also check the list of poisonous plants (see page 27), and make sure none of them is in the bird room.
Stove burners: Fatal burns may result if the bird lands on a burner that is still hot.	Put covered pots of cold water on hot burners not in use. Never let a bird fly unsupervised in the kitchen.
Candlelight: Bird can be fatally burnt if it flies through the flame.	Do without candlelight while the bird is flying free.
Wastebaskets, ornamental vessels: Bird may slip in and starve to death or suffer a heart attack caused by panic because the bird cannot get out again.	Use woven baskets, or line the inside with wire mesh. Fill ornamental vessels with sand.
Direct sun, overheated car: Bird may suffer heart attack caused by heat stroke.	Make sure the bird can escape into the shade; air the car.
Stoves, electrical appliances: Bird may be burned, possibly fatally.	Install them in such a way that the bird cannot get near them.
Temperature fluctuations: Abrupt changes to either heat or cold cause heat stroke or colds.	Let the bird adjust gradually to temperatures lying between 41° and 86°F (5° and 30°C).

Mutual preening is best of all.

(see "Plants in the Bird Room," page 27) in the middle of the tub.
• Plant three or four branches or bamboo sticks about 6 feet (2 m) long and 1¼ inches (3 cm) thick vertically around the smaller pot, and secure them there with wire.
• Fill the space between the outer and the inner pot with smaller stones and earth, and spread a layer of bird sand on the top.
• Connect the vertical branches with horizontal ones 10–16 inches (25–40 cm) long and of varying thicknesses at several levels, tying them in place with raffia. Not all of them have to be level, since part of the purpose is to encourage the bird to climb.
• Attach a little bell, a wooden ring, and a tassel of raffia to different cross branches so that they are at about eye level for the cockatiel. The best place is near a fork in a branch, because cockatiels like to sit in such places.
• Replace the branches and raffia ties every three to four weeks, just as you do in the cage.

My tip: Don't let the ends of the perching branches extend beyond the rim of the outer tub. In this way you can ensure that the droppings will land in the bird sand instead of on the floor.

Where to Put the Bird Tree

Of course, the bird tree has to have a permanent place in the room. It is best located as far from the cage as possible, so that the bird has to fly back and forth every time it wants to eat or drink; this exercise is healthful

cause everything growing there is exposed to exhaust fumes, and these poisonous substances penetrate into the wood. Even branches from parks and woods have to be rinsed off well with hot water and let dry before a bird comes into contact with them, because pollution and acid rain are everywhere.

My tip: Recently pet stores have started carrying natural branches—a godsend to city dwellers.

How a Bird Tree Takes Shape

• Place a few heavy rocks in the bottom of a huge flower pot or a tub to ensure stability.
• Place a somewhat smaller flower pot with a nonpoisonous, viny plant

In order to scratch its head, a cockatiel has ▶ to raise its foot between the wing and the body.

It is essential that a human surrogate partner pay plenty of attention to the bird. This means spending a lot of time close to it, whistling tunes for it, talking to it, and playing with it or providing things for it to play with.

for it. When birds are young and enterprising, they need hardly any urging to fly. But as they get older, cockatiels are likely to prefer leisurely walking to flying—a tendency that, for their health's sake, should not be encour-

This cockatiel is nibbling very gently on the hand of its human partner. Interaction like this helps build mutual trust.

This ladder structure is sturdy enough for a cockatiel and is an ideal place for the bird to perch when you want to let it be near you outside the "bird room."

aged. Near a window is a good place for the bird tree, because there the bird will get enough daylight and will be able to watch other birds passing by outside.

A Birdproof Room

Even a conscientious bird keeper will probably not be able to eliminate all conceivable dangers that lurk in a room shared by birds and human beings. You think you know all your birds' habits and peculiarities, and then one day you find them doing something completely different and dangerous. Cockatiels are particularly attracted to electric wires. They like to bite them and can easily get electrocuted. For this reason you should run all wires under rugs or protect them with metal pipes. The birds' desire to find nesting cavities can also prove dangerous. Thus I couldn't find my

cockatiel Lucy one day. She was nowhere in sight and didn't make a peep. I was sure she had not escaped because the window and the porch were screened. Becoming anxious, I got down on my hands and knees to check under all the furniture and in all the corners—nothing. I thought I had looked everywhere, opened all drawers and closets. The only item I had neglected to check was the partially open grand piano. In desperation, I played a few notes because the sound of the piano always attracted Lucy. To my amazement she came hissing out of her hiding place—the resonating sound box of the piano, which she must have assessed as an acceptable nesting cavity.

The Greatest Danger: Flying Away

I have watched an escaped cockatiel fly away rapidly under the open sky four times, each time filled with a mixture of admiration and of sadness—knowing that there was no way to save these glorious birds. A cockatiel that has found its way to freedom quickly covers distances that make it unlikely that its owner can recover it. Adapted in nature to a nomadic existence, cockatiels in Australia have no need to orient themselves by salient features of the landscape. An escaped cockatiel, lacking this sense, can thus be saved only when exhaustion, hunger, or chill prevents it from flying on. If it is not found quickly then, it will either fall victim to a predator or die of weakness. Anybody aware of this scenario will take all conceivable precautions against the bird's escaping.

The first and foremost rule is to keep windows and doors closed or screened at all times. A cockatiel may escape even from its closed cage if, through patient work of its strong beak, it succeeds in opening the cage door. Check the lock on the door. If it opens easily, add a small padlock. Curtains in front of an open window will not keep a bird from flying off, for it may climb up on them, bite a hole in the material, and squeeze through just for the fun of it. That is why at least one window should be equipped with a strong wire screen or hardware cloth having spaces of ⅜ × ⅜ to ¾ × ¾ inches (1 × 1 to 2 × 2 cm). Stretch the screening on a wooden frame, which is then screwed tightly to the window frame. This way you can air the room anytime, and the bird will have plenty of fresh air in the summer.

Plants in the Bird Room

House plants can be dangerous to cockatiels if the plants are poisonous or contain substances that don't agree with the birds. It would be folly to assume that a cockatiel will ignore such a tempting opportunity to gnaw; on the contrary, the bird is bound to explore all plants to see how suitable they are for gnawing and may poison itself in the process.

Poisonous and injurious house plants: A cockatiel should have no contact with the following plants: poison primrose, *Strychnos nux-vomica,* catheranthus, crown of thorns, all *Dieffenbachia* species, yew, hyacinth, periwinkle, all nightshades, narcissus, oleander, berries of *Ardisia* plants, poinsettia, variegated laurel, the berries of ornamental asparagus, rosary pea, caladium, elephant's ear, and azalea.

Although the following plants are not poisonous, they contain substances that irritate the mucous membranes and can therefore be very harmful for as small a creature as a cockatiel: ivy, *Monstera,* flamingo flower, Chinese evergreen, amaryllis, crocus, philodendron, and *Schefflera.*

Caution: A cockatiel can injure itself—especially its eyes—on cacti and other plants with spiny parts.

Important: When you buy indoor plants, always ask whether they are safe for birds. Florists and nurseries keep offering new species and varieties which are not included in the above lists.

Nonpoisonous plants: These present no problem and can be in the room for both your and the bird's pleasure. It is always possible, though, that your cockatiel may take a special liking to one or another of them and get carried away thinning it.

Variety is the Spice of Life

In the wild, cockatiels keep busy foraging for food, performing parental duties, and finding and preparing nesting cavities. They are not, to be sure, constantly occupied with these tasks and take resting periods and short naps periodically, but on the whole their lives are far from monotonous. It is important, therefore, for cockatiels living in captivity to have a

This scene depicts a minor disagreement. The threatening stance of the cockatiel on the left will soon convince the other one to give in.

The gray cockatiel would like its pearled friend to scratch it.

ing shapes and thicknesses also provide the bird's feet with healthy exercise. Another beneficial aspect of a bird tree is that it diverts the bird's interest away from plants and other objects in the room. The cage and the bird tree will soon become the bird's favorite "hangouts." Still, your cockatiel will be delighted to have something new now and then to focus its attention on, and pet stores sell all manner of toys to satisfy this need. But even the most ordinary household items are a welcome novelty in the daily routine.

Wooden toys, such as a ring to swing on or a little ladder, are popular with the birds, but so are wooden curtain rings and empty thread spools.

Metal mirrors are of interest to cockatiels kept singly because the reflection in the shiny metal is taken for another bird.

A small brass bell on a short, strong chain should always be present both in the cage and in the bird tree.

Cockatiels like **paper** and **cardboard.** They like to nip little bits off the edges and let them drift to the floor like confetti.

Thick cords (see drawing, page 30) are an invitation to climb and perform acrobatic tricks.

You can easily fashion raffia into **bushy tassels.** Your cockatiel will keep pulling pieces out of the tassel, but it usually takes several days before the tassel is destroyed.

Aaron, an amazingly articulate male cockatiel I used to have, loved paying daily visits to my desk. There he found things he could see his reflection in, paper to gnaw on, and, above all, pencils, which he adored. But since I could not let him chew on the lead, I always had a second pencil container ready to substitute. It contained short elderberry sticks, which Aaron happily reduced to splinters. If my mother came to see my while

chance to use their beaks, to climb and play, and to perform acrobatics, so that several hours each day are spent "doing things."

Favorite Activities and Playthings

A bird tree provides the most natural opportunity for exercising the beak and maintaining physical agility. The perching branches of the tree lend themselves to being gnawed and contain substances like minerals and trace elements that help keep the bird healthy. Twigs and branches of vary-

The pied cockatiel is keeping its eye on the photographer, while the yellow one is stretching.

Aaron was keeping me company, he would immediately fly to her head, perch there, and remove all the hairpins from her chignon. When her hair cascaded down, he would exclaim delightedly, "Whadda ya know!"

The Importance of Being Included

You will no doubt soon notice that your cockatiel is beginning to feel more and more at ease in its new home and is moving around in it quite naturally. A bird is amazingly adept at conveying what it likes, doesn't want, and is afraid of. Thus it may be frightened of the vacuum cleaner. If so, warn your cockatiel before vacuuming. Bring the machine into the room and explain to the bird that it had best retreat to its cage or the bird tree. Carry it there on your hand before you plug in the vacuum. In this way the bird will gradually overcome its fear.

If nothing upsetting is going on, your cockatiel will be most content if it can sit close to you and watch whatever you are doing. If some things it can exercise its beak on are available, the bird's happiness will be complete.

A cord hanging from the cage ceiling is used by cockatiels primarily to keep the beak busy. Some also like to practice climbing on it.

Sometimes, though, your cockatiel feels the need to make noise. In this mood one of its favorite activities is to shove objects with its beak across the tabletop and over the edge, watching—and listening to—them crash to the floor. Make sure nothing you value gets broken, and let the bird have its pleasure.

Cockatiels Can Learn to Obey

If from the very beginning you consistently say, "No, no!" whenever the bird wants to hack at you or is about to get into trouble of some other sort, the message will eventually get across. Aaron, for instance, was determined to inspect the telephone cord. Luckily he got onto my desk only when I was there, so I could always stop his attacks with a "No, no!" Whenever I had to leave my birds alone, I unplugged the telephone.

All my resident cockatiels also learned to respond to my command to climb over my hand into the cage. Only a visiting bird named Charlie obstinately refused to do this. For him I devised a trick. I would get Laura into the cage, close the door, pick up the cage, and pretend to leave the room. Charlie would immediately fly to the top of the cage with a loud scream that demanded to be let in. There was nothing worse to him than to be separated from Laura.

Vocal Talents

Lonely, neglected cockatiels can turn into annoying screamers, but a happy cockatiel often uses its voice to imitate all kinds of sounds. Some cockatiels have a real talent for whistling. I knew one bird that whistled Strauss's "Radetzky March" better than I could ever hope to do it. Charlie didn't attempt anything more ambitious than "Lightly Row," and all

Aaron was interested in was to duplicate the neighbor's dog whistle. On the other hand, Aaron learned to say quite a few short phrases and often made us laugh. Lucy inevitably greeted me by saying "There you are!" Aaron was fond not only of the telephone cord, as already mentioned, but also of telephone conversations. If someone called, he always came up and pressed his head as close to the receiver as possible. Sometimes he also entered the conversation. On one memorable occasion I got quite an attractive job offer over the phone. Aaron immediately piped up in a loud voice: "Not interested, not interested." Those were the words he used when I offered him food he didn't like.

A Short Course for Encouraging the Talent for Speech

Cockatiels with a talent for speech repeat many things they hear frequently, and they enjoy doing it. If your bird shows no interest in speaking, you should whistle to it often; perhaps your cockatiel has a talent for whistling. Here are some ways to encourage vocal mimicking:
• Say a word or phrase appropriate to a certain situation whenever that situation arises, or invent a sequence of whistled notes as a substitute for words. For instance, say "Good morning" whenever you enter the room in the morning, and "Good night" before you turn off the lights in the evening.
• Say a short phrase, using a consistent rhythm, whenever the bird looks at you expectantly.
• Sing or whistle the same simple tunes for your bird several times each day.
• As often as you can, go over the entire repertoire during a quiet half hour. Try to find time for this every day.
• Whenever you try to teach your bird

Schedule of Chores

Daily

Remove all droppings from the corn cob in the cage and the tub of the bird tree with a spoon. Add some fresh corn cob.

Empty all food dishes and, if you use one, the water dispenser; wash with hot water, dry well, and replenish. Fill seed cups only half full.

Scrub dirty branches with an old toothbrush or sandpaper and wipe with a damp cloth.

Check in the afternoon whether there is enough birdseed left. If a lot of empty hulls are covering up seeds, skim off the hulls with a spoon. Don't blow them off; doing that makes too much dust.

Twice a week

Wash the bottom of the cage and the corn cob tray with warm water, dry well, and supply fresh corn cob.

Throw out leftover seeds. Rinse all food cups with hot water, dry, and fill again.

Monthly

Spray the cage with warm water, removing all traces of feces with a cloth; wooden parts can be rinsed with hot water. Dry everything well with a cloth.

Replace old, gnawed twigs and branches inside the cage and on the bird tree with fresh ones that have been washed with hot water and dried well.

Whetting or rubbing the beak keeps it clean and strong.

Many cockatiels regard a bell as a kind of surrogate partner because it has a "voice," moves, and reacts in different ways when nudged.

something new, let it sit on your hand. The best time is dusk, when there are few visual distractions. Now introduce the new word or phrase.

Cockatiels Are Intelligent

The intelligence of cockatiels cannot be compared to that of gray parrots, cockatoos, amazons, or macaws, all of which are amazingly smart. But cockatiels can easily compete with parakeets, which, along with jackdaws, ranked next in intelligence tests devised by the Viennese ethologist Professor Otto König. In other words, cockatiels are less intelligent than gray parrots and yellow-fronted amazons but brighter than common ravens and pigeons.

There are many things that will make you realize how clever your cockatiel is. For instance, when you approach the cage, the bird is usually able to tell from your face if you are going to close the door.

A Second Cockatiel

Lucy was my first cockatiel. I got her very young, and she became friendly after just a few days. She liked to spend a long time on my shoulder when I played the piano, and when there was music on the radio, she performed little dances. She didn't talk much, but when the phone rang, she would always say, "Hello, Wolter's residence." If I had to leave her alone for a few hours or a whole day, she would retreat into a corner, lie rather than sit on the floor, and stay there until I returned. I felt so sorry for her that I brought Aaron home to keep her company. Lucy was about a year old at the time and first looked at Aaron with skeptical curiosity. But when he squatted down in front of her and begged for food, she knew what to do: she fed him. During the next few weeks they adjusted to each other

without special difficulty, and a few months later Aaron successfully wooed her with his courtship displays, though they never produced offspring. Unfortunately a second cockatiel doesn't always get such a friendly welcome. Sometimes it takes several weeks for the first bird to accept the presence of a newcomer. The already established bird keeps the initially unwelcome companion at a distance by hissing and hacking at it. To help both birds, the keeper should exercise caution when introducing a second bird.

Introducing a second bird

● It makes little difference what sex the second bird is. If both are males, or both females, one of them will automatically fall into the role of the missing sex. But the newcomer should be very young (10–12 weeks), so that the older one will respond to it in a parental manner.

● You should keep the new bird in a cage of its own, if possible, for at least a week, and spend a lot of time with it, to help it get over its fear of you.

● When you combine the two cockatiels, leave both cages open, so that the birds can get away from each other if a fight develops.

Hygiene Is Necessary

Like all pets, cockatiels produce dirt. Their droppings, however, are quite harmless. If some droppings land on a hard, smooth surface, wipe them off with a tissue immediately; if they land on cloth, let them first dry thoroughly, then sweep or vacuum them off. The hygiene required for the bird's well-being is a little more time consuming

A courtship display can hardly be more ▶ *impressive than this one. If the bird on the left is in fact a female, she will no doubt soon surrender to the male's wooing.*

A cockatiel has no difficulty scratching its head— though the maneuver may seem a bit awkward.

and involves chores that have to be done regularly, or the bird may get sick (see "Schedule of Chores," page 31). The cage, the bird tree, and all accessories have to be kept clean. The best thing to do is to draw up a regular cleaning schedule.

Important: Don't use detergents or other cleansers. These are poisonous for birds. Water at a temperature of about 130°F (55°C) will do the job and doesn't present any dangers.

What to Do With the Bird During Vacation or If You Get Sick

Traveling with the bird: If you want to take your bird along, you have to consider not only your own preferences but also the bird's needs when you arrange for accommodations. Traveling abroad is out of the question because of the strict entry regulations for members of the parrot family.

A cockatiel can survive a trip by car, but you have to make sure there are no drafts, even in the summer. If you stay in a hotel, the bird must remain in its cage for its own safety because the cleaning personnel will not keep doors and windows closed. This also means that the bird may be exposed to drafts when the room is cleaned. Spending time in a tent or camper is not something you should impose on your cockatiel. If you rent a cottage, on the other hand, there will be a homelike atmosphere that your bird can enjoy.

Leaving the bird at home: Your cockatiel will be happiest if it can stay in its familiar environment—assuming that a reliable caretaker takes care of its needs twice a day and lingers a little to talk with the bird.

Boarding the bird: Perhaps you have friends or relatives willing to take in the bird while you are gone. If so, be sure to give them all the necessary information, such as the telephone number and address where you can be reached, and the veterinarian's phone number. Also make sure you give them everything the bird needs, and check that it will be able to fly free in its temporary quarters.

Pet stores and veterinarians will sometimes board cockatiels for a small fee. But there your bird will not be able to fly.

In case of illness: If you have to go to the hospital, either in an emergency situation or for some planned treatment, I recommend that you make arrangements for your bird as suggested above. A person living alone should, while healthy, think about what would happen to his or her bird if its owner got sick and look for a reliable caretaker ahead of time.

My tip: Animal shelters often have names and addresses of bird lovers willing to share their homes with one or two birds either for a vacation or in an emergency. Get in touch with such a person ahead of time, so that you can make arrangements quickly if necessary.

The Proper Diet

The Natural Diet of Cockatiels

Wild cockatiels living in Australia find half-ripe seeds, the most important component of their diet during breeding and rearing time, only after rainy periods. The rest of the year they live mostly on the fully ripened seeds of various grasses and other plants, wild cereal grains, and—if they find themselves near cultivated fields—on ripe wheat kernels. Professor Immelmann has also observed cockatiels imbibing flower nectar in eucalyptus trees. Cockatiels drink water from rivers and watering holes, where they congregate in great numbers. If there is a drought, however, they have to get along with the dew that falls in the morning in the steppes.

Birdseed as the Staple

Birdseed mixtures for parrots—of which the cockatiel is one—are composed of varying proportions of different kinds of millet and of canary grass seed, rape seed, buckwheat, oats, black and white sunflower seeds, safflower seed, hemp seed, and wheat kernels. Such a mixture contains all the carbohydrates needed, enough fat, protein, and minerals, and some vitamins.

Important: Always check the date of packing, which is stamped on the box or bag. It should not be farther back than eight months because there is no knowing how long the seed was stored before packaging. All the seeds and grains you buy are harvested once annually and, if stored properly, will stay viable for one year and re-main edible during the second year. But since the nutritional value gradually declines even under proper storage, you should test them by sprouting them (see "Sprouting Recipe," page 38). Seeds that germinate are high in vitamins; if only a small portion sprouts, most of the mixture is nutritionally useless and should be discarded.

Signs of Spoilage

● Decay: Rotting seeds have a penetrating odor, whereas healthy ones don't smell.
● Mold: If you see a whitish gray film on some of the seeds, the food is moldy. But you have to look closely to detect the mold.
● Vermin: If seeds are clumped together and have cobweblike filaments emanating from them, the presence of vermin is indicated.

Cockatiels like to snitch food from the family table if they get a chance. But not everything that tastes good is healthful for a bird. For this reason you should have a piece of apple or some cooled, boiled potato ready for your pet.

A cockatiel doesn't pick up food in its "hand" the way large parrots do. But it does hold onto a spray of millet or a piece of fruit with its foot to bite off pieces.

Two cockatiels that are used to each other

. . . don't fight over food;

Important: If there is the slightest sign of spoilage, don't under any circumstances go on feeding the mixture to your bird.

Proper storage: If you have only one or two cockatiels, a package of birdseed will last for several weeks. During this time you should store the birdseed like grain for your own consumption, namely, in a dry, dark, and airy place. It is best to put the birdseed in a bag made of natural fibers and hang it in an appropriate place.

How Much Birdseed a Day?

• Put two tablespoons of seed in the food cup in the morning; if you have two cups, put one spoonful per cup.
• Skim off the empty husks in the early afternoon or toward evening;

otherwise the bird won't be able to get at the seeds underneath.
• If the birdseed is almost gone in the evening, give another scant spoonful so that the bird will find some food first thing in the morning, when it will need fuel for the new day.

It is appropriate to make sure that the bird has food available at all times. This is particularly important when you go out. You might someday be delayed or prevented from coming home, and then full food dishes would be a godsend.

It is not right to try to keep the bird from getting obese by rationing the birdseed. Birds have a high rate of metabolism and need to eat small amounts of food frequently. Obesity is a problem only for birds that are fed

instead they peacefully share a treat like this millet spray.

an inappropriate diet, lack sufficient exercise, and don't have enough to do.

Drinking Water

Your cockatiel should, of course, get fresh drinking water every day. Ordinary tap water is fine. If you want to provide an especially healthy drink, buy the so-called bird drink that pet stores sell. Noncarbonated mineral water with the ingredients listed on the label is even better. Only sick birds need boiled water, weak black tea, or camomile tea, if the veterinarian prescribes it.

Vegetables and Fruit

Wild cockatiels always eat fresh seeds, whereas our pet cockatiels have to make do mostly with older seeds and grains. To make up for this, your bird should get plenty of fresh vegetables, wild plants, and fruit. This is important for the bird's overall health, and it keeps the plumage in good condition. In addition, fresh fruits and vegetables are a good insurance against weight gain. Produce is especially rich in vitamins if it has been grown locally and brought to market shortly after picking rather than being transported over long distances. Still, exotic nonlocal fruits like bananas, figs, kiwis, oranges, and tangerines can always be included to add variety to a bird's diet. The best guiding principle for choosing fresh things for your cockatiel is to consult your own menu and to share everything that is not harmful for the bird.

37

Drinking water stays clean in a dispenser because hardly any dirt can get into the small drinking cup. When you buy a water dispenser, make sure it is designed to hang from horizontal bars.

Raw vegetables: Give your bird eggplant, endive, fresh peas, young dandelion greens, a few kernels of fresh corn, Swiss chard, carrots, lettuce that has not been sprayed, sorrel, spinach, zucchini.

Fruit: Your cockatiel will enjoy raw pineapple, apples, apricots, bananas, pears, blackberries, strawberries, raspberries, fresh figs, tangerines, mangoes, melons, oranges, cherries, peaches, grapes.

To be avoided: All kinds of cabbage, raw and green potatoes, green beans, lettuce that has been sprayed with pesticide, grapefruit, rhubarb, plums, lemons.

Important: Nothing should be fed to birds directly from the refrigerator. Everything should be at room temperature and have been washed in warm water, dabbed dry, and, if applicable, peeled.

How to Offer Fresh Food

Foods that are of solid consistency, like pineapple, apples, pears, carrots, and zucchini, are cut into slices thick enough to be stuck between the cage bars. Soft fruits are cut into small pieces, mixed with berries, peas, shredded leafy vegetables, and perhaps grated vegetables, and placed on a flat dish. Don't be disappointed, however, if your cockatiel fails to recognize that the dish contains delicious food. The bird may do nothing more than touch a few pieces with its beak. If a bit of fruit juice gets onto its tongue, it will probably take a second taste. But it may take days or even weeks before a cockatiel really starts eating the fresh food. You can help the process by eating pieces of the same fruits or vegetables in the bird's presence. That is likely to arouse its curiosity.

Don't be uspet if the bird doesn't eat the way you think it should. It will probably pick out only tiny bits of fruit, grind pieces of leaves between its beak, and actually swallow very little. Even so, particles of the fresh food are absorbed and provide vitamins.

Minerals and Trace Elements

Birds, like human beings, need only minute amounts of these substances, and both birdseed and fresh food supply some. The most important minerals, namely, calcium and phosphorus, are contained in the mineral stones or cuttlebone given to birds to whet their beaks on, as well as in bird sand. When you buy a mineral stone, be sure it says somewhere on the label that the stone contains all the substances necessary for skeletal growth and for the formation of feathers.

My tip: Cuttlebone, which is sometimes given to birds instead of a mineral stone, should not be offered to females that are broody because it causes egg binding in some of them.

Sprouting Recipe
- Cover ½ teaspoon each of birdseed, oat kernels, and wheat kernels with ¾ inch (2 cm) of lukewarm water and soak for 24 hours.
- Rinse the seeds with lukewarm water and let drain; then place in a glass dish and let sit lightly covered for 48 hours in daylight and at room temperature.
- As soon as sprouts appear, you can give the seeds to the bird. In another 24 hours the sprouts will have grown larger and will contain more vitamins.

Important: Always rinse sprouts with lukewarm water and drain well before feeding them to birds.

When the wings are fully extended, the white bands on them stand out on the back. This posture is part of the courtship display and is the equivalent of a declaration of love.

Herbs and Weeds

Fresh food, which we have already discussed, should include herbs and weeds because these are similar to the plants cocktiels find in the wild.

Your **kitchen and garden** can supply basil, chervil, and parsley to add to the bird's fresh food.

In **meadows** (unfertilized) and along country paths (not along roads with car traffic because of the exhaust fumes) you can pick wild plants when you are out walking. Look for ripe and half-ripe seed heads of annual bluegrass and wild millet, leaves and flowers of vetch, daisies past blooming and without stems, open seed cases of pansies, flowers and leaves of hawthorn, leaves and stalks of young dandelion, sorrel, chickweed, shepherd's purse, and watercress.

How to serve: All herbs and wild plants should be rinsed with lukewarm water, shaken dry, and attached in small bunches to the cage roof with a clip.

My tip: If you notice your cockatiel trying to "bathe" in the damp greens, offer it a bath right away or a shallow bowl with leaves for a "dew bath" (see page 17).

Things That Add Variety to the Bird's Menu

Items available at pet stores

• Spray millet is the most important "extra" and is usually what birds like the best. A highly nutritious and unadulterated natural food, it is ideal for breeding birds and their brood, as well as for sick and weakened ones. Healthy, adult cockatiels should get no more than about a 2-inch (6-cm) piece a day.

• I'm in favor of adding vitamin supplements to the birds' diet because there is no way to measure the vitamin content of birdseed or of plants and fruit. Vitamins are crucial to health, and the smaller an organism, the more sensitively it reacts to shortages. For this reason I recommend adding vitamins to the drinking water during the winter or, if a bird habitually eats very little fresh food, throughout the year. Pet stores and drug stores sell multivitamins. Be sure you check the expiration date; old vitamins are of no benefit.

• Pet stores also sell treats in the shape of hearts, rings, and sticks covered with seeds that are stuck on with a honey solution. Because of this sweet adhesive, however, these treats are very high in calories. Fresh twigs keep the beak just as busy and are much better for your bird's health.

What you can provide yourself

• The yolk of a hard-boiled egg mixed with a little low-fat cottage cheese is a very valuable form of protein. One teaspoonful a week will benefit your cockatiel's health.

• If you use freshly cracked cereals for your breakfast, you can give your cockatiel barely a teaspoonful a day, soaked in a little lukewarm water.

• To prevent any deficiency condition, you should give your cockatiel seed sprouts every day for several four-week periods: during the winter, in early spring, during molting, at breeding and nesting time, and any other time when very little fresh food is available. The birdseed mixture used as the basic staple can be sprouted, as well as oat and wheat kernels sold especially for sprouting at health food stores. As soon as viable seeds start absorbing water, a chemical reaction takes place that results in germination. This process releases vitamins that increase the nutritional value of the seeds and grains as they swell, and even more as they sprout.

Very important: Don't cover sprouts airtight, or they will get moldy. Uncovered sprouts, on the other hand, dry out quickly. For this reason sprouts the bird doesn't eat within two hours should be disposed of.

Snitching at the Table

Many cockatiels love to snitch food from the table. However, this is not without danger for the bird. It may scald itself on hot food or burn its tongue, or it may eat something that doesn't agree with it. If you are going to let your bird share your family's meals, you will have to keep a constant eye on it and have some suitable food ready for it, such as a boiled, cooled potato, a few cooled noodles, a little piece of bread, or some fruit.

The Most Important Points at a Glance

What is good for the bird

• A dishful of mixed birdseed daily.

• A piece of spray millet about 2 inches (6 cm) long daily.

• Fresh vegetable and fruit daily if possible.

• As often as possible, a bunch of fresh greens, either cultivated or wild.

• A regimen of sprouts daily about every 4 to 6 weeks.

• Fresh drinking water daily.

What is bad for the bird

• Cold food that comes straight from the refrigerator.

• Rotting or moldy food, even if the bad spots have been cut away. Mold and rot continue to spread far below the surface where they are not visible.

• Foods containing salt and spices; also sweet and fatty things.

• Alcoholic beverages and coffee.

Not to be considered: Depriving the bird of food with the idea that a very hungry bird will "eat out of your hand." This is cruelty to animals.

Please remember: Give fruit in small pieces, or offer it somewhere where it cannot be budged and the bird can take bites off it. A cockatiel can properly taste things like strawberries, cherries, and grapes only if they are held for it and, preferably, cut in half.

This practical millet-spray holder should be hung from the cage ceiling in such a way that the bird can peck at the millet from all around while sitting on a perch.

Spreading the wing and tail feathers is always indicative of physical comfort.

What to Do If Your Bird Gets Sick

A Sick Cockatiel

It is easy to tell a sick bird by its behavior. It hardly moves at all, avoids other birds, sits on its favorite perch apathetically with somewhat puffed-up plumage, and often buries its beak in its back feathers. With half-shut eyes it barely follows what is happening in its immediate vicinity. It rests on both feet, not on one the way healthy birds do when sleeping, with the other foot tucked into the abdominal feathers. A sick bird hardly eats, often doing not much more that stir around in the seed dish with its beak. It may, however, drink a lot. Its posture is not upright as usual; instead the body is closer to a horizontal position, with the tail drooping downward. If a sick bird is not quickly helped, it may get so weak that it is no longer able to hold onto its perch and ends up squatting on its belly on the cage bottom (see drawing on right). You can't deliberate long whether or not to take the bird to the veterinarian because when such a small creature gets sick it needs help quickly.

What you can do for the bird: Make sure everything is quiet around the cage, and provide even warmth. A sick bird needs a cage of its own and should be given lukewarm camomile tea to drink. Quite often, exposure to an infrared heat lamp is beneficial (see page 44).

The Trip to the Veterinarian

If your cockatiel's health doesn't improve within a few hours, you should take the bird to the vet the day you notice something wrong, or on the very next day at the latest. If you observe any major signs of alarm (see table on right), you must take the bird to the veterinarian immediately. Many cities have veterinary clinics that are open for emergencies even at night and on holidays. In exceptional cases the vet may pay a home visit, but usually you have to take your pet to the office or clinic.

Please remember to do the following:
- Line the bottom of the cage with clean paper instead of sand so that the vet can immediately tell the consistency of the droppings.
- Protect the bird from cold, dampness, and heat on the trip. The best way is to wrap the cage in a blanket or put it into a big carton, but make sure enough air can get in.

Not all veterinarians who treat pets have had much experience with cockatiels. For this reason it is important to find out while the bird is in good health where in your area there is a vet with the requisite background. Often an experienced pet dealer can steer you in the right direction.

A sick cockatiel that is squatting weakly on the bottom of the cage should be taken to a veterinarian as soon as possible.

Health Problems at a Glance

What you Notice	Cause for Alarm if Combined with the Following Symptoms:	Possible diagnosis: Requires Veterinary Treatment
Apathy, avoidance of contact (can be temporary indisposition)	Staggering, trembling, falling off perch	Possible infection
Refusing to eat (can be temporary indisposition)	Convulsions, even if only partial	Vitamin deficiency, tumor
Feeding regurgitated food to objects (may be courtship display with surrogate object)	Tossing off slimy discharge; sticky feathers; gummed-up nostrils	Crop inflammation
Labored breathing, frequent yawning (possible causes: lack of exercise, obesity)	Squeaking or whistling sound when breathing; bird hooks bill on cage bar and hangs down to breathe through straight windpipe	Pnuemonia, thyroid problems
Frequent sneezing (possible causes: dry air, cleansers)	Runny discharge from nostrils	Bad cold; early stage of some other disease
Mushy or runny droppings for more than 1–2 hours (possible causes: agitation, cold food, cold bathwater, change of environment, loneliness, sadness)	Foamy, noticeably discolored excrements; diarrhea	Serious sign of alarm! Symptoms of many diseases
Hard, unsuccessful straining in attempt to pass excreta	Cries of pain	Constipation; intestinal obstruction; in females, possibly egg binding
Limping, dragging one leg, drooping wing (possible causes: bruising caused by collision)	Leg or wing hangs down limply	Fracture
Bulge under the skin or on preen gland		Tumor or other kind of growth
Bleeding from cloaca or from wounds		Internal bleeding; broken blood vessel
Restless picking through the feathers, constant scratching (possible causes: nervousness)	Weight loss; dull plumage; feather plucking	Mites or other parsites; emotional disorder
Spongy, brownish growth on beak, cere, or feet		Tiny mites, contagious to bird partner (mycosis of beak)
Significant loss of feathers (see "The Molt," page 46)	Permanent molt; bare spots on body	Mites; inadequate nutrition; hormonal problems
Upper mandible too long; overgrown claws	Interferes with eating; toes get caught	Requires correction

Questions the Vet May Ask

- How old is the cockatiel?
- When did it first look sick to you?
- What have you noticed in particular?
- Has the bird been sick before?
- If so, who treated it, what medications were used, and what was the diagnosis?
- What birdseed mixture is the bird eating? (Be sure to bring along a sample.)
- What does it drink?
- What fruits and vegetables has it been eating recently?
- Might it have nibbled on something poisonous?
- What other animals live in your household
- Is any person in your household sick?

Talking with the Veterinarian

In most cases the droppings can be analyzed either right away or by the next day. If the result does not lead to a conclusive diagnosis, the veterinarian will use his or her judgment and suggest shots or medication. Ask to have everything explained to you in detail, especially if a biopsy of the skin, the mucous membranes, or internal organs is suggested. Ask specifically whether the proposed treatment is absolutely necessary, what chance of success it offers, whether it will cause the bird pain, and whether there are any other methods of treatment. Also ask what the likely consequences would be if you should opt against the proposed procedures.

If Medications Have to Be Given

If medications are required, follow the directions of the veterinarian exactly concerning dosage, length of treatment, and method of administration. Liquid medications and powders are sprinkled on the birdseed or added to the drinking water (tablets are crushed first). If drugs are added to the water, make sure the bird has no other way of satisfying its thirst as, for instance, by getting at a dripping faucet or eating fruit and vegetables. If it is necessary to force-feed the medication, wrap a towel loosely around the bird and press the bird gently against your body in such a way that its head is bent back slightly. Then dribble the required amount into the beak next to the tongue.

Use of an Infrared Heat Lamp

Set up a lamp with a 150- to 250-watt infrared bulb about 16 inches (40 cm) away from the cage in such a way that the rays penetrate into only half of the cage. With this arrangement your bird can get away from the heat source if it gets too hot. Make sure the bird has enough drinking water available while the lamp is on, and place a bowl with steaming water near the cage to raise the air humidity. Leave the infrared light on for two days, then turn it off for a day. If necessary, turn it on again after this break. If the bird seems obviously better, gradually move the lamp away from the cage so that the temperature doesn't drop suddenly. Make sure the bird is kept evenly warm afterwards, and avoid all drafts.

Ornithosis (Psittacosis)

In earlier days ornithosis, then known as psittacosis, was dreaded because it can spread to human beings and because it was sometimes fatal. Now there are effective drugs against it that work for humans as well as birds if treatment is initiated early enough. If was because of psittacosis and Newcastle disease that quarantining (minimum 30 days) was instituted

This is the correct way to trim overgrown claws. Make sure you don't cut into the blood vessels, which are barely visible inside the translucent nail. If you hold the claw up to a light, you will be able to see the blood vessels better.

Cockatiels are said to be the fastest flyers of all Australian birds.

for birds belonging to the parrot family entering the country. People thought at that time that parrots were the only birds that contracted psittacosis. Today we know that native wild birds as well as poultry can get psittacosis. For this reason the disease is now generally no longer called psittacosis (Psittacidae = parrot family) but is known as ornithosis (from Greek *ornithos,* bird).

Signs of the disease: There are no characteristic symptoms. Birds with the disease are apathetic, produce soft droppings—often with traces of blood—have the sniffles, and suffer from shortness of breath. They often have conjuctivitis with a slimy discharge from the lower eyelids. These symptoms can occur singly or in combination.

Treatment: See the veterinarian immediately! A laboratory analysis of the feces can tell definitively whether the bird has ornithosis.

Ornithosis has to be reported to a veterinarian or the U.S. Public Health Service.

Misshapen Feathers

Signs of the disease: Large wing and tail feathers, as well as small contour feathers, remain stuck in the sheaths enveloping them, with only a small, brushlike tuft unfolding. Instead, the feathers may taper halfway up and twist around the shaft. Misshapen feathers are seen mostly in older cockatiels. Often the crest is affected; feathers may fail to grow back in after the molt or are malformed or undersized and soon fall out again.

Possible cause: Generally viruses are to blame, but malformation of feathers can also be caused by nutritional deficiencies, hormonal imbalances, poor circulation, or cysts in the feather papillae.

Treatment: Whatever you think the cause may be, take the bird to a veterinarian experienced in treating birds.

Feather Plucking

Very few cockatiels acquire this bad habit, which plagues mostly the larger parrots.

Signs: The bird keeps pulling out feathers until bare and bloody spots appear.

Possible causes: Many ornithologists see unhappiness as the cause of this compulsive, self-destructive behavior. Others think that in the course of preening themselves some birds become addicted to the liquid inside the feather shafts.

Treatment: Unfortunately there is no effective way to cure this condition. Chances for improvement are best if feather plucking is linked to an emotional state—as when it first starts during the owner's absence, and decreases or stops when the owner returns and pays a lot of attention to the bird. However, in most cases the cause is not so obvious and the plucking is associated with other health problems. A cockatiel that plucks its feathers should be taken to a veterinarian who specializes in treating birds.

The Molt

The molt is not a disease, but for older cockatiels it represents a strain on the physical system. During this period birds should be given an especially nutritious diet and kept evenly warm, quiet, and undisturbed. In the course of molting many feathers are shed and replaced. Depending on their size, new feathers take a few days to one or two weeks to grow back in. A bird pecks at its plumage more than usual at this time, but in a way that is clearly different from normal preening. If the molt is particularly severe, a bird may be temporarily unable to fly. If this happens, some sturdy sticks, appropriately set up, will help your bird reach all its favorite spots by climbing.

The Droppings

The droppings are a good indicator of a cockatiel's state of health. A healthy bird passes droppings about every 15 to 20 minutes. Normal droppings are soft but not shapeless, and are never runny. But cockatiels are very sensitive and react to the most minor events with a change in the consistency of the droppings. Sometimes the excrements are watery after the bird has bathed or if it has been momentarily frightened. They can also be very soft after the consumption of a lot of fresh food. In a healthy bird, however, the droppings return to normal within a few hours. If the consistency remains soft to watery for more than a day, spread some activated charcoal over the birdseed. If you notice sliminess or blood in the droppings, this is cause for serious alarm.

When a bird gets too warm, it opens its beak to cool down.

The beak and cere of this bird are infected with mycosis.

If Your Birds Have Babies

Where Is the Bird Family Going to Live?

If you hope for offspring from your cockatiels, keep in mind that you will have to house the bird family for approximately 12 weeks. While the baby birds are still in the nest box, the cage the parents are used to will do. Once the young birds fledge, however, they don't return to the nest box again, although they are still fed by their parents for at least two weeks. During this time they need adequate flying space. For this reason it is preferable to invest in the largest indoor aviary you can find or, if the climate is suitable, in an outdoor flight 6 feet (2 m) long with an attached shelter. Set up a nest box there, and move the prospective parents into the aviary.

Do You Have a True Pair?

If you bought your cockatiels as young birds, you will be able to tell after one year whether you indeed have a male and a female. A bright orange cheek patch is a sure sign of the male sex. The female has light markings on the under tail-coverts, a feature not found in males.

The Right Age for Breeding

Although cockatiels reach sexual maturity at about nine months, they should not be allowed to have young until they are one year old. Younger birds lack the necessary skills for parenting. Even if the eggs are fertile and they are incubated, the baby birds usually die within a few days because the parents haven't learned yet how to feed them properly.

The Right Nest Box

Pet stores sell nest boxes for cockatiels in two shapes; one kind is taller than wide, the other squatter. Bird fanciers who are handy with tools can build the boxes themselves.

What the nest box should look like: The floor should be made of hardwood about 1½ inches (3.5 cm) thick and should measure 15 by 10 inches (38 × 26 cm). The lid, which is the same size and should flip open, and the side walls can be made of thinner softwood. The sides should be 15–18 inches (38–46 cm) high. The entry hole needs a diameter of a little over 3 inches (8 cm), and there should be a perch or a narrow board below it for the birds to land on. The birds also need a horizontal perch running lengthwise inside the box. The nest hollow, about 4¾–6 inches (12–15 cm) wide, is located on the side opposite the entry hole. In upright boxes some kind of aid for climbing should be added below the entry hole.

Litter: Place about 1½ inches (4 cm) of damp peat moss and some sawdust in the bottom of the box. This makes it easy, after the chicks have hatched, to remove the droppings daily and add a little more litter.

Mounting the nest box: Hang the box on one of the aviary or cage walls at a height that allows you to look into it now and then without difficulty.

A nest box should ideally measure about 10 × 15 × 18 inches (25 × 38 × 46 cm). Cockatiels raise broods successfully, however, even in somewhat smaller boxes.

The orange cheek patch begins to show up after 18 days.

Wooing and Courtship Display

If you have a chance to observe a small flock of cockatiels in a large outdoor flight, you can witness how pairs of birds come together and form a life-long bond. Of exceptionally complacent nature, cockatiels live together amicably in flocks and tolerate even related species like Stanley or Western Rosella (*Platycercus icterotis*) parrots and parakeets. Unpopular members of the flock are ignored but hardly ever chased or attacked. Hostile encounters between birds that don't know each other occur only under crowded conditions, but even then injuries are rare. Single males look for suitable mates within the flock. In an aviary, however, where there are no unmated birds, a cockatiel may court an already claimed female and is then subject to attack from the female's partner because a rival must always be driven away.

If two previously unattached cockatiels of opposite sex take a liking to each other, they first express their feelings by perching close together. If one of them inches even closer and the other doesn't move away, this is tantamount to an "engagement." From now on the two will always be together, eating, sleeping, and preening at the same time. Soon the male begins to touch the female cautiously with his beak, gradually working up his courage to gently scratch her head. Then, one day, he emits his courting song, a melodic and rhythmic whistling that confirms the bond that has been forming. He also drums with spread wings and often with his beak, sounding almost like a woodpecker tapping on wood, to impress the female. Sometimes he circles her several times in a row, taking tiny steps, raising his crest, and slightly spreading his wings. At other times he flies through the room in shallow loops, performing artful turns when veering around. Landing next to his chosen one again, he bows deeply before her with spread wings and tail and whistles at the same time.

Matrimony

The female shows no sign of being impressed by the male's courting, but eventually she will settle down close to her partner in a horizontal position with her tail pointing sideways, inviting him to mate. He now climbs onto her back and lays his tail across hers in such a way that their cloacas touch (see drawing on right), allowing his sperm to penetrate to her sexual organs and fertilize the eggs. During copulation the birds emit soft squeaking or melodic gurgling sounds. Sometimes the male produces a soft growl that has a soothing quality. After the birds separate, they shake themselves and start preening. If the pair has already spent some time in the nest box before mating, the first egg will now soon appear there. At intervals of two days more eggs are laid, until there is a clutch of four to six eggs, weighing ⅕–¾ ounces (5–7 g) each.

My tip: Occasionally cockatiel females that are kept singly lay eggs, which are of course not fertilized. Let such a female sit on her eggs until she gets tired of doing so. In this way she can act out her frustrated urge to brood. If you remove the eggs, the female usually goes on laying and needlessly weakens her body.

When the male mounts the female to mate, the cloacas of the two birds touch, thus making fertilization of the eggs possible.

Although cockatiels reach sexual maturity at 9 months, it is better not to let them breed that early. At this age they often fail to perform their parental duties adequately. By the time they are about 12 months old, they should be able to incubate the eggs and raise their young without problems.

Both Parents Brood

With cockatiels, as with cockatoos, both parents take turns incubating the eggs, something other members of the parrot family don't seem to do. Feeding the female is therefore not part of the regular courtship ritual with these birds, although the male will occasionally offer his mate food. The birds begin to brood after the second egg is laid. The female sits on the eggs at night; the male, during the day. But both birds often stay in the nest box together and often leave it together to eat or stretch. The baby birds hatch after 21 days, emerging in the order in which the eggs were laid. The parents should be disturbed as little as possible during the incubation period and be given lots of fresh food (see "The Proper Diet," page 35).

Important for Successful Incubation

• During the brooding period the birds need quiet, an even temperature of around 72°F (22°C), fresh air, and an air humidity of 60 percent. If the birds are kept in a heated room, run a humidifier there or set up vessels full of water well covered with wire mesh.

This cockatiel chick is about 18 days old. If it feels threatened, it raises its crest, hisses, and rocks from side to side.

• When checking the nest, always wait until both birds have left the box. Brooding cockatiels are extremely aggressive and will use their beaks even on familiar human beings.
• Hold the eggs up to a light bulb: fertile eggs have a bluish opaqueness and look darker than infertile ones, which are light and translucent.
• Remove infertile eggs only if there are more than four eggs in the clutch. Too obvious a change can upset the birds and result in their giving up brooding.
• Don't wipe off or wash eggs that are dirty. Doing so could harm the embryos. The eggs are covered with a natural, waxy layer that protects the embryos from infections.
• Once the chicks have hatched, check the nest every day because chicks occasionally die. Decomposition sets in quickly and will endanger the other nestlings. Prompt removal is therefore important.
• For the first few days after hatching, the nestlings produce only small amounts of droppings. As they grow bigger, however, the nest gets quite dirty and presents a health hazard to chicks as well as parents. Therefore, about six days after the first chick has hatched, start to take the nestlings out gently—in the parents' absence—and put them in a small basket lined with tissues, remove the droppings from the nest, add some fresh litter, and then return the chicks. Do this every day.
• If the parents take it into their heads to stay with their young when you are ready to clean the nest, they will hiss at you angrily. In this case, drive them away gently with a small stick. They will leave the box and watch you, protesting vociferously.
• Keep giving the parent birds rearing food (available at pet stores) and plenty of fresh food (see page 38) during the nestling period.

With cockatiels, both parents sit on the eggs and feed the nestlings. Once the young leave the nest, they are still fed for a while, primarily by the father, while the mother begins to lay a new clutch.

Development of the Young Birds at a Glance

1st to 3rd day: A chick weighs 0.14–0.18 ounce (4–5 g), is about 1¼ inch (3 cm) long, has closed eyelids, and is covered with sulfur-yellow down. The head is naked, and the skin, beak, cere, feet, and claws are a pale pink color.

4th day: The eyes begin to open.

5th day: Chicks weigh about ½ ounce (15 g). They beg food from the parents with a "tsitt, tsitt" sound.

10th day: The eyes are now fully open. The first quills appear. Chicks can hold up their heads, take little steps, and hiss audibly.

11th day: Chicks weigh 1.3 ounces (37 g). The tip of the beak turns dark.

12th day: The egg tooth is shed.

15th day: Nestlings weigh 1½ ounces (45 g). Upper and lower mandibles become hard.

18th day: The cheek patch begins to appear. When sensing danger, the chicks raise their crests, spread their wings, and hiss.

21st day: Nestlings weigh a little over 2 ounces (60 g). The yellow down feathers are replaced by permanent gray ones.

28th to 35th day: Nestlings now weigh close to 3 ounces (80 g). The plumage is fully formed but more muted in color than that of the parents. The young birds now leave the nest box and are able to fly.

38th to 42nd day: The young birds begin to eat independently but are still fed, mostly by the father, for another 2 weeks.

48th day: The large feathers have become fully keratinous.

3rd to 4th month: The first molt occurs. The beak turns dark gray.

8th to 9th month: The young birds are now sexually mature, and the plumage has adult coloration.

Understanding Cockatiels

Things a Cockatiel Can Do

As you get used to having a cockatiel around the house, you begin to realize just how cleverly the bird deals with many different situations and how it masters difficult tasks even though its living conditions differ drastically from those prevailing in its natural habitat. For example, a cockatiel sitting in its cage may stare at the cage door for hours at a time. It already understands that the door is the way to freedom but that it has to be open.

Mutual preening—especially of the head area—not only serves a hygienic function but also strengthens the pair bond.

Some day it will systematically investigate the door with its beak and conclude correctly that the lock needs further exploration. Depending on the effectiveness of the locking mechanism, many cockatiels succeed in opening the door, and they retain this fact in their memory.

Here is an example of the inventiveness of cockatiels. A bird I know was left alone frequently but was allowed to move freely around a very large room that contained a climbing tree with many branches. The room was connected, without a door, to a staircase leading to a higher floor. The staircase had a brass railing. Attracted by the shiny metal, the cockatiel often sat on the railing and pecked at it. It also liked walking slowly up the railing. At the top it would usually fly right back to the bottom and start walking up again. But one day it stayed at the top for a minute, then turned sideways and started sliding down, standing on both feet. It obviously enjoyed the fast ride, and since then sliding has been part of its daily routine.

My cockatiel Lucy invented a kind of merry-go-round. On the cockatiels' climbing tree there was a fairly long rope about ¾ inch (2 cm) thick, on which the birds enjoyed climbing. Lucy would fly to the lower end of the rope, seize hold of it, and flap her wings to turn in circles many times. When the rope became quite short because it was wound so tightly, she would stop flapping and let herself be twirled

In flight the white wing bands are particularly conspicuous.

around and around until the rope straightened out again. Aaron always watched with great interest but never tried to imitate this trick.

Several cockatiel breeders I know told me independently of one another that their birds would all call and scream for hours or even days when another bird had escaped. In some cases the escapee was lured back by the calls, whereupon the racket stopped instantly. If a bird died, however, the others would not raise their voices but tended to be quieter than usual.

All these stories show that cockatiels are equipped with many abilities, abilities that are necessary for living in the harsh environment of their native Australia. Body language, vocal utter-

What the Crest Conveys

If the crest feathers lie flat with only the tips pointing upward, the bird is in a quiet, contented mood.

If the crest is raised vertically, the bird is alert, interested in its surroundings, and ready for action.

If the crest points straight up with the tips of the feathers leaning slightly forward, the cockatiel is in a state of great agitation.

If the scene giving rise to the agitation takes on a frightening aspect, the bird whips its crest straight back, hisses threateningly with head raised high, and wavers between wanting to attack and wanting to flee.

ances, and sensory capacities are used not only to make peaceful coexistence in the flock possible but also to ensure survival in a world that is fraught with dangers and often offers only scant food resources.

Typical Body Movements

Stretching the legs: Every so often a cockatiel feels the urge to stretch, which it does by extending one leg and the wing of the same side backward. When the leg is retracted, the toes are often curled up. These motions are performed to counteract fatigue after staying in the same, not quite balanced, position for a long while.

Standing on one leg: Stretching the legs is often followed by pulling one leg up into the abdominal plumage, although stretching is not necessarily a prelude to pulling up the leg. A bird rests standing on one leg when it feels relaxed and is not active. A cockatiel generally also pulls up one leg when it sleeps.

Burying the beak in the back feathers: Cockatiels are flexible and able to twist their heads around 180 degrees (see drawing, page 11). They need this ability in order to preen themselves, an activity for which the beak has to reach all parts of the body. They also twist their heads 180 degrees to bury their beaks in their back feathers when they rest, a position many cockatiels assume for sleeping.

Lifting the wings: Both wings are raised in closed position. This is another form of stretching. Birds also lift their wings when they are too warm; this helps get rid of excess heat.

Raising wings sideways: The fully extended wings are stretched sideways as part of the male's courtship ritual. At the same time the male bows his head deeply, often making the whole body dip steeply forward. If your cockatiel assumes this posture in front of you, you can safely interpret it as a declaration of love.

Typical Activities

Preening: A cockatiel spends a total of at least two hours a day preening itself. In the course of the day it draws each of its many feathers through its beak, oiling it, smoothing it, and removing all dust and dirt in the process. The oil comes from a gland hidden in the feathers at the base of the back just above the tail. From this oil or uropygial gland the beak extracts a fatty substance and distributes it all over the plumage. The head, however, is rubbed directly over the gland because the beak is of no use in grooming the head. The most a bird can do is scratch its head with its toes. To do this, the foot is not raised directly to the head but is passed upward underneath the wing.

Shaking the feathers: Several times a day a cockatiel suddenly shakes its feathers so vigorously that an audible rustling sound is produced. This concluding gesture gets rid of whatever dust may still be left after preening and at the same time returns each feather to its proper place. But other activities and moods also end in a shake of the feathers. If, for instance, the bird has been following some human action either nervously or curiously, it will shake itself as soon as the tension lets up.

Twitching of the facial feathers: The yellow feathers on the face and forehead, which form the so-called mask, can be momentarily and partially raised, creating the impression of a nervous twitch. You can observe this when the bird is mildly irritated, perhaps by a noise or an annoying light.

Whetting the beak: After every meal, and often without having eaten at all, a cockatiel rubs its beak against the bars of the cage, or better yet, on a perch. This action serves to clean the beak and keep it in good shape. That is why it is so important that the bird have plenty of natural branches available. A cockatiel will also whet its beak in a gesture of greeting when you return after a prolonged absence. If you respond by scratching on the same surface with your fingernail, the bird will feel as though it is among its own kind.

Yawning: Cockatiels yawn, as we do, but usually because of an oxygen shortage rather than fatigue. Birds kept indoors are very sensitive to stale air. If you see your cockatiel yawn, you should air the room well.

Sneezing: Sometimes cockatiels make a sneezing noise. But sneezing doesn't serve the same function as it does for us; cockatiels sneeze to clear their nasal passages. Sneezing is no cause for worry. If a bird has a cold, it has a runny nose.

Whistling, calling, screeching: Many bird lovers complain about the loud and often shrill voices of cockatiels. This complaint may at times be justified in the case of aviary birds, but pet birds are excessively noisy only when they feel lonely and don't have enough to keep them busy. Usually, screeching birds are poor creatures that are kept singly and have spend all their time in the cage. If a pet bird feels happy, its vocal contact with the human beings who are part of its world or with others of its own kind is pleasant, never grating. People whom the bird knows well are usually greeted with a joyful call, whereas their exit from the room evokes a plaintive, disappointed tone. Many cockatiels answer when they are called. They respond either with the contact call a bird uses toward a mate sitting on a different perch, urging it to come, or, in the case of a single cockatiel, with a special whistling sound. When birds fly, they often emit a short flight call that consists of two syllables. Very rarely, you will hear a high-pitched, one-syllable alarm call. Cockatiels can also effectively hiss in situations of danger or rivalry with other cockatiels, and even nestlings already know how to hiss.

Cockatiels choose the tops of tall trees as resting places.

Sensory Capacities

Sight: Cockatiels perceive the world in color, just as we do. This is not surprising, for the different colors many birds display in their plumage have definite functions in avian coexistence. Cockatiels also have "panoramic" vision because their eyes are located on the side of the head, providing a wide-angle view that allows them to spot predators at a great distance and to make their escape. The area taken in by both eyes simultaneously is smaller than in human beings. On the other hand, cockatiels can absorb well over 100 images per second, while the human eye processes only 16. For a bird that flies fast, recognizing things at high speed and in detail is very important.

Hearing: The hearing of all birds is extremely acute. After all, they have to communicate with each other over large distances by means of calls and songs. Their hearing is also very differentiated, that is, they can discriminate between small differences in frequency. This ability is essential for reacting properly to the various vocal utterances they encounter.

Taste: With birds that live exclusively on seeds and nectar, taste doesn't play any significant role. Baby birds learn from their parents what is edible and then eat those things. Pet cockatiels, on the other hand, develop definite dislikes for some foods and become almost addicted to others. Probably the birds' taste sense develops in response to the varied foods offered them in captivity.

Smelling: Not much is known about the olfactory sense of birds. It is clear, however, that any kind of smoke accumulation is disturbing to cockatiels. Even cigarette smoke has caused my cockatiels to twitch nervously and utter audible "hmm" sounds. If possible, avoid smoking near cockatiels.

A flock of cockatiels traverses the Australian steppe in rapid flight.

Life in Nature

Cockatiels come from Australia, where they live in the interior of the continent. They penetrate to coastal areas only if scarcity of food forces them to do so, and they avoid dense forests. But they are not dependent on a specific habitat. They are found in open eucalyptus savannahs and in steppes covered with mulga shrubs, as well as in desertlike grasslands covered with spinifex grass. Conditions can be extremely harsh. There may not be any rainfall at all for months at a time, and the temperature often is 100°F (38°C) in the morning, rising to 113°F (45°C) or higher by noon. Cockatiels rest in the midday heat in groups of up to 50 birds in the tallest trees or bushes they can find. They prefer dead branches and tree limbs to perch on, where the gray of the wood provides good camouflage for their gray plumage. They always sit parallel with the branch, so that their silhouettes don't stand out and thereby attract the attention of birds of prey.

In the morning and evening cockatiels fly long distances to drink. They are extremely uneasy on the ground, however, and always land, not on the shore, but in the shallow water, where they take a few hasty sips and then quickly fly off again. Sometimes there are flocks of thousands of cockatiels near a watering place. They circle above the water for a while, then descend rapidly, dropping to the water at an almost vertical angle. The birds forage for food on the ground in the early morning hours and in the late afternoon, remaining very quiet. During the dry seasons they eat the seeds of various grasses and other plants, and they pick up some sand to aid digestion. Cockatiels also drink nectar, preferably from eucalyptus blossoms. If there is too long a period without rain, the birds take off in large flocks and travel hundreds of miles until they find a place that has food and water.

Australia's Fastest Flyer

Cockatiels have the reputation of being the fastest flying birds of Aus-

tralia. They fly at an even speed, fast and straight. While flying, they sometimes emit their two-syllable flight call. The white areas of the wings are clearly visible when the cockatiels fly and probably play a role in flock cohesion. When the birds want to land, as at a watering place, they let themselves drop straight down, slowing their fall only shortly before they reach ground. The undulating flight typical of other small parrots is not seen in cockatiels.

Predators of Cockatiels

Raptors are the natural predators of cockatiels. Living in open landscapes, cockatiels therefore choose high places for perching so that they can scan wide areas of the sky. The birds' nervousness on the ground arises from the fact that they cannot see far amid grass and shrubs. In recent times cockatiels have acquired a new and dangerous enemy in Australia, namely house cats, that were imported and have become feral. Unfortunately, nature has not equipped the birds with a warning system that works against predators on the ground. In addition, starlings, which have been introduced into Australia, compete with cockatiels for nest sites. These pesky birds are not intimidated by the hissing of cockatiels, and they usually win contests over nesting sites, even when a pair of cockatiels is already sitting on a complete clutch. But the biggest threat to cockatiels is drought, which sometimes lasts for years. Cockatiels respond to drought by taking up a nomadic way of life, a form of existence for which they are amazingly well adapted.

Brooding Is Done When It Rains

If you take into consideration the long dry periods in central Australia and the fact that cockatiels can ade-

Description of Cockatiels
(*Nymphicus hollandicus*)

Family: Psittacidae
Subfamily: Psittacinae
Geographic origin: Australia
Habitat: Steppes with scrub growth, semideserts, and locations along creeks (that is, shallow streams with intermittent flow) all over the continent
Wild strain: Light to dark gray with a white band on the wings, a yellow mask, a red cheek patch, and a small crest
Length of body: 11½–13½ inches (29–34 cm)
Length of tail: 5½–6¼ inches (14–16cm)
Weight: 2.8–3.5 ounces (80–100 g)
Life expectancy: 15–20 years
Sexual maturity: At 8–10 months
Eggs per clutch: 4–6, sometimes more
Egg laying: One every other day
Beginning of incubation: After the second egg is laid; sometimes after the first egg
Length of incubation: 19–21 days
Nestling period: 32–35 days

quately feed their young only when there are plenty of half-ripe seeds, you will understand better why these birds may produce up to three or four broods, one after another, during a single rainy period. It may be a year or more before conditions conducive to breeding will recur. If in the course of their wanderings cockatiels come across areas where it rains, their urge to breed is immediately awakened. The males launch into their courtship displays and show their mates possible nesting cavities. If a female rejects the first suggested site, the male keeps looking until he finds one that meets with her approval. Holes in dead tree limbs are preferred, but in breeding areas there is a lot of bird activity because innumerable parakeets also use the rainy season for breeding. Therefore many cockatiels make do with nesting cavities that are open at the top. Cockatiels don't collect nesting materials. But in the course of improving the site—for example, making a deeper hollow for the eggs, smoothing the inside of the cavity, and enlarging the entry hole— enough debris is produced to cover the nest hollow. Like our pet cockatiels, wild females lay one egg every other day. If there is an abundant food supply, a clutch may contain as many as seven eggs. The male broods during the day; the female, at night. The partner that is not sitting on the eggs uses the free time to gather food and guard the nest, staying very close to it.

If the rain is steady, the moisture makes grass and other plants sprout within a few days. By the time the young hatch after 21 days, there is plenty of the half-ripe seed that growing nestlings need. The droppings in the nest are eaten or carted off and then consumed by insect larvae and a certain kind of ant. The development of young cockatiels in the wild is the same as that of cage or aviary birds.

Life in the Flock

By the time the fledglings leave the nest they are able to fly, and once they're out they don't return there. By imitating their parents, they gradually learn how to gather food for themselves, though they continue to be fed. Once a new brood is underway, however, parental care for the existing young grows more and more sporadic as the parents become increasingly absorbed in their new tasks. Still, the parents feel responsible for their older offspring for about two weeks after they leave the nest. All the juveniles of a breeding area that are left to fend for themselves come together in a band, build up their physical skills by climbing and taking extensive flights, and thus discover the world they live in.

When it rains, the birds can be seen hanging upside down from branches with wings spread wide. They are enjoying a rain bath, for when they drink at watering places they are always in a hurry and don't feel safe enough to bathe there.

Living together in a band, the young birds also practice social behavior patterns that are inborn but need to be tried and tested.

First courtship attempts: Even before the juvenile birds finish their first molt at about nine months, they begin to practice courtship rituals. The young males show the young females possible nesting sites, and each suitor keeps trying to get as close as possible to a chosen female. If the latter isn't attracted to the wooing male, she won't let him stay close but drives him away by pecking at him. If, on the other hand, she accepts his presence, an "engagement" is not far off.

Although the young males already perform the courtship displays typical of their species, mating is delayed until after full sexual maturity has been achieved, a time that coincides more or less with the post-juvenile

Some ornithologists class cockatiels with cockatoos because the species have two things in common: Both have crests, and in both the male and the female share in incubating the eggs and in caring for the young.

Cockatiels like to use natural branches as perches.

molt. Meanwhile, the "engagements" already formed remain intact. Mutual preening and constant seeking of each other's company are outward signs of the bond.

Renewed nomadic journeys: When vegetation is getting scarcer and it becomes necessary to look for new, more hospitable places, the large breeding communities break up into smaller groups of up to 50 birds. Families stay together within these groups. Young birds that have formed pair bonds stay together for life and find some group to join. Young birds that are still "unattached" may find mates when meeting other cockatiel groups. Most birds, however, are paired up by the time they again find a rainy area and thus don't have to waste precious time on exploratory courting.

How Cockatiels communicate with each other: Cockatiels recognize each other not only as members of the same species but also as belonging to the same group and as mates, that is, as distinct individuals.

Vocal communication takes the form of calls, the different meanings of which the birds have learned to recognize since birth. In the contact call, for instance, they not only hear the question "We're here, where are you?" but also can tell, by fine nuances in sound, which bird is calling. These vocal nuances are of special importance during the active breeding phase. At that time it is crucial for the cockatiels to live closely together in the breeding grounds without eruptions of aggression and at the same time to respect and maintain the privacy of individual pairs.

Expertly Written Manuals For Premium Pet Care!

"Clear, concise...written in simple, nontechnical language."–Booklist

Great News for Pet Owners!

Cockatiels
A Complete Pet Owner's Manual

Cockatoos
A Complete Pet Owner's Manual

With a Special Cha
Understanding Coc

Canaries
A Complete Pet Owner's Manual

With a Special Chapter:
Understanding Canaries
—Plus 36 Full-Color Photos

BARRON'S

Lovebirds
Matthew M. Vriends
A Complete Pet Owner's Manual

With a Special Chapter:
Understanding Lovebirds

BARRON'S

BARRON'S

PET OWNER'S MANUALS

African Gray Parrots (3773-1)
Amazon Parrots (4035-X)
Bantams (3687-5)
Beagles (3829-0)
Beekeeping (4089-9)
Boxers (4036-8)
Canaries (4611-0)
Cats (4442-8)
Chinchillas (4037-6)
Chow-Chows (3952-1)
Cichlids (4597-1)
Cockatiels (4610-2)
Cockatoos (4159-3)
Dachshunds (2888-0)
Doberman Pinschers (2999-2)
Dwarf Rabbits (3669-7)
Feeding and Sheltering
   Backyard Birds (4252-2)
Feeding and Sheltering
   European Birds (2858-9)
Ferrets (2976-3)
Gerbils (3725-1)
The German Shepherd Dog (2982-8)
Golden Retrievers (3793-6)
Goldfish (2975-5)
Gouldian Finches (4523-8)
Guinea Pigs (4612-9)
Hamsters (4439-8)
Killifish (4475-4)
Labrador Retrievers (3792-8)
Lhasa Apsos (3950-5)
Lizards in the Terrarium (3925-4)
Longhaired Cats (2803-1)
Lovebirds (3726-X)
Mice (2921-6)
Mutts (4126-7)
Mynahs (3688-3)
Parakeets (4437-1)
Parrots (2630-6)
Persian Cats (4405-3)
Pigeons (4044-9)
Ponies (2856-2)
Poodles (2812-0)
Rabbits (4440-1)
Rottweilers (4483-5)
Schnauzers (3949-1)
Sheep (4091-0)
Shetland Sheepdogs (4264-6)
Shih Tzus (4524-6)
Siberian Huskies (4265-4)
Snakes (2813-9)
Spaniels (2424-9)
Tropical Fish (2686-1)
Turtles (2631-4)
Yorkshire Terriers (4406-1)
Zebra Finches (3497-X)

Paperback, 64-80 pp., 6½" x 7⅞",
over 50 illustrations including more
than 20 full-color photos in each
ISBN PREFIX: 0–8120

Index

Color photos are indicated in **boldface** type.

Bird Associations
American Cockatiel Society, Inc.
1801 19th Avenue, N.E.
Minneapolis, MN 55418

National Cockatiel Society
Route 1, Box 412
Equality, AL 36026

American Federation of Aviculture,
 Inc. (AFA)
P.O. Box 56218
Phoenix, AZ 85079

The Avicultural Society
Warren Hill, Halford's Lane
Hartley Wintney, Hampshire RG27
 8AG
Great Britain

The Canadian Avicultural Society
32 Dronmore Court
Willowdal, Ontario M2R 2H5
Canada

Magazines
American Cage Bird Magazine
One Glamore Court
Smithtown, NY 11787

The AFA Watchbird
2208 "A" Artesia Boulevard
Rendondo Beach, CA 90278

Bird Talk
P.O. Box 6050
Mission Viejo, CA 92690

Bird World
Box 70
North Hollywood, CA 91603

Cage and Aviary Birds
Prospect House
9–13 Ewell Road
Cheam, Surrey SM1 499
Great Britain

Books
Cooke, Dulcie, and Freddy Cooke.
 Keeping and Breeding Cockatiels.
 Blandford Press, London, New
 York, Sydney, 1987.
Forshaw, Joseph M. *Australian*
 Parrots, 2nd edition. Lansdowne,
 Melbourne, Australia, 1981.
Low, Rosemary. *The Complete Book*
 of Parrots. Barron's Educational
 Series, Inc., Hauppauge, New York,
 1989.
Vriends, Matthew M. *The New*
 Cockatiel Handbook. Barron's
 Educational Series, Inc.,
 Hauppauge, New York, 1989.
———. *The New Bird Handbook.*
 Barron's Educational Series, Inc.,
 Hauppauge, New York, 1989.

Important Note:
 People who are allergic to feathers or feather dust should not keep birds. If you think you may have such an allergy, consult your doctor before acquiring a bird.
 Ornithosis (also called psittacosis) is at this point quite rare in cockatiels (see page 44), but it can give rise to life-threatening conditions in both human beings and cockatiels. For this reason you should take your cockatiel to the veterinarian if you suspect it may have contracted the disease (see pages 42 and 44) and call your own doctor if you yourself have cold or flu symptoms. Be sure to mention that you keep a bird.

Pleasures and Responsibilities of Keeping Cockatiels
 Annette Wolter, the cockatiel expert of Barron's Series of Pet Owner's Manuals, explains how to keep cockatiels properly so that they will stay healthy and become friendly. Includes much practical advice on housing, care, and nutrition. Also suggestions on how to play with cockatiels and keep them occupied. With 28 fascinating color photos.
 Also suitable for children who want to take care of their own cockatiels.

All inquiries should be addressed to:
Barron's Educational Series, Inc.
250 Wireless Boulevard
Hauppauge, NY 11788

Library of Congress Catalog Card Number
90–26490

International Standard Book Number
0-8120-4610-2

**Library of Congress Cataloging-in-
Publication Data**

Wolter, Annette.
 [Nymphensittiche. English]
 Cockatiels : how to take care of them and
understand them / Annette Wolter ; color photo-
graphs by Karin Skogstad and outstanding
animal photographers ; drawings by György
Jankovics ; consulting editor, Matthew M.
Vriends.
   p.   cm.
 Translation of: Nymphensittiche.
 Includes index.
 ISBN 0-8120-4610-2
 1. Cockatiel.   I. Vriends, Matthew M., 1937-
II. Title.
SF473.C6W64   1991
636.6'865–dc20
                              90-26490
                                CIP

PRINTED IN HONG KONG

1234   4900   9876543